# DAVID SUZUKI'S GREEN GUIDE

# DAVID SUZUKI & DAVID R. BOYD

# DAVID SUZUKI'S

# GREEN GUIDE

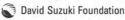 David Suzuki Foundation

GREYSTONE BOOKS
DOUGLAS & McINTYRE PUBLISHING GROUP
Vancouver / Toronto / Berkeley

Greystone Books
A division of Douglas & McIntyre Ltd.
2323 Quebec Street, Suite 201
Vancouver, British Columbia · Canada v5T 4S7
www.greystonebooks.com

David Suzuki Foundation
219–2211 West 4th Avenue
Vancouver, British Columbia · Canada v6K 4S2

*Library and Archives Canada Cataloguing in Publication*
Boyd, David R., (David Richard)
David Suzuki's Green guide / David R. Boyd and David Suzuki.

Includes index.
ISBN 978-1-55365-293-9

1. Environmental protection—Citizen participation—Handbooks, manuals, etc.
2. Sustainable living—Handbooks, manuals, etc. 3. Green products—Handbooks, manuals, etc.
I. Suzuki, David, 1936– II. Title. III. Title: Green guide.
TD171.7.B69 2008    363.7'052    C2008-902674-8

Editing by Nancy Flight
Copy editing by Barbara Tomlin
Cover and text design by Jessica Sullivan
Printed and bound in Canada by Freisens
Printed on acid-free paper that is forest friendly (100% post-consumer
recycled paper) and has been processed chlorine free
Distributed in the U.S. by Publishers Group West

We gratefully acknowledge the financial support of the Canada Council for the Arts,
the British Columbia Arts Council, the Province of British Columbia through the Book
Publishing Tax Credit, and the Government of Canada through the Book
Publishing Industry Development Program (BPIDP) for our publishing activities.

*This book is dedicated to every person*
*worried about the Earth*
*who has ever wondered "What can I do?"*

# Contents

● ● ●

# Acknowledgements

•ɔ    •ɔ    •ɔ

Thanks to all the good people at the David Suzuki Foundation and Greystone Books for supporting this book. In particular, we are grateful to Rob Sanders, Nancy Flight, Ann Rowan, Dominic Ali, and Barbara Tomlin. We would also like to thank all of the colleagues, friends, and family who reviewed parts of the manuscript and provided gentle but constructive criticism. And finally, a special thank you to Margot and Meredith for putting up with David B.'s obsession with reducing his family's ecological footprint during the months of research and writing for this book.

# DAVID SUZUKI'S GREEN GUIDE

# 1

# Help Wanted:
# Join the Sustainability Revolution

*Imagination is more important than knowledge.*
ALBERT EINSTEIN

"What can I do?" This is the question people inevitably ask when thinking about today's environmental problems—the climate crisis, declining biological diversity, and toxic pollution. It's a short and simple question, but there's no easy answer (which is why we wrote this book). Everything we do has some kind of impact, but some decisions and actions are more important than others. Nearly all of us want to do the right thing when it comes to the environment, but few of us have the time or the specialized knowledge necessary to sift through the competing claims and mountains of information about the greenest choices. It can be confusing when we hear media reports suggesting:

- There's still scientific debate about the cause of climate change (there's not).
- It's more eco-friendly to drive to the store than to walk (it's not).
- It's fine to buy a gas-guzzling Hummer rather than a hyper-efficient hybrid Toyota Prius (ridiculous).

This book cuts through the fog, identifying the most important actions we can take and how to get started. Knowledge plus motivation equals action.

## THE ECOLOGICAL FOOTPRINT

For many people in North America, caught up in the trials and tribulations of day-to-day living, the state of the world's climate, oceans, forests, soils, rivers, wildlife, and wetlands may seem remote. Yet the basic biological reality is that humans are still utterly dependent on the natural world and its ecological processes for our health, well-being, and prosperity. All humans need to breathe, eat, and drink, and it's nature that provides us with fresh air, clean water, and the ability to grow food. All humans require a reasonably hospitable climate, and the interconnected web of natural systems regulates the planet's climate and makes life on earth viable.

A prime example of this dependence is our reliance on insects for pollination of food crops. Indigenous people relied exclusively on wild species for pollination. Today, however, honeybees originally taken from Europe to North America pollinate about one-third of the crops eaten by Americans. These crops, ranging from almonds and apples to soybeans and strawberries, have a value of $15 billion annually. Various environmental problems, including the introduction of parasitic mites, caused a 50% decline in honeybee colonies between 1971 and 2006. Now the introduced honeybees are experiencing a sudden population crash labeled colony collapse disorder, causing additional losses of 30% to 70%. Although the cause of the problem is not known with certainty, various human disruptions are the prime suspects. Native North American bees are also experiencing extinctions, extirpations, and population declines. Decades ago Albert Einstein reportedly warned "If the bee disappears from the surface of the earth, man would have no more than four years to live. No more bees, no more pollination, no more plants, no more animals, no more man." Today there are still no technological alternatives to animal pollinators.

While our individual actions may seem insignificant when viewed in isolation, the cumulative impact of billions of apparently benign actions is devastating. Scientists at the University of British Columbia in Canada created a concept called the ecological footprint in an effort to illustrate the connections between individual actions and global consequences. The ecological footprint measures how big a chunk of the planet is needed to produce the resources for, and assimilate the waste of, one person for a year. Ecological footprints include the dimensions of land and water required to produce crops, livestock, fish, wood products, and energy, as well as the area required to absorb the carbon dioxide produced by burning fossil fuels. The size of our individual ecological

## AN APPLE'S ECOLOGICAL FOOTPRINT

CONSIDER two seemingly similar apples. One apple grew on a tree in your backyard using nothing but sunshine, compost, and rainfall, relying on natural processes to avoid diseases and pest infestations. When the apple was ripe you simply picked it and ate it (or made apple pie). The other apple grew on a commercial farm in another country. This apple was grown in soil that required chemical fertilizers and irrigation to nourish the tree. Pesticides made from fossil fuels were used to battle pests and diseases. Large machinery powered by dirty diesel fuel was used on the farm, along with migrant labor. The apple was waxed, packed in a box, and shipped thousands of kilometers to your country (using more energy and generating more emissions). Then it was trucked to a distribution center and eventually to a store. All along the line, the apple was refrigerated to keep it fresh, using yet more energy. You drove to the store to purchase groceries and returned home, where you ate this second, noticeably less tasty apple. The local apple obviously requires far fewer resources to grow, harvest, transport, and store. By using less energy, it causes less pollution. In short, the local apple has a much smaller ecological footprint than the imported apple.

footprint depends on where we live, what we eat, how we travel, and other ways that we use energy and consume resources. You can estimate your ecological footprint at www.myfootprint.org.

TABLE 1. *Average ecological footprints (hectares)*

| | |
|---|---|
| United States | 9.6 |
| Canada | 7.6 |
| Australia | 6.6 |
| U.K. | 5.6 |
| Europe (EU-25) | 4.8 |
| Middle East and Central Asia | 2.2 |
| Latin America | 2.0 |
| China | 1.6 |
| Asia Pacific | 1.3 |
| Africa | 1.1 |
| GLOBAL AVERAGE | 2.2 |

Globally, the average ecological footprint for all of humankind is 2.2 hectares (5.5 acres) per person, although there are wide variations between and within nations (see Table 1). This seemingly small number, 2.2 hectares, may not appear to be problematic (a hectare is a square area where each side of the square is approximately the length of a football field). However, the Earth has a limited quantity of biologically productive areas—cropland, pasture, forest, lakes, rivers, wetlands, and oceans. Given the planet's current population of 6.5 billion people, there are only 1.8 productive hectares per person available globally. The ecological bottom line is that humanity's footprint exceeds the Earth's capacity by about 25%. The Earth's remarkable regenerative capacity can no longer keep up with our demands. People are turning resources into waste faster than nature can turn waste back into resources. We're no longer living off the annual interest provided by the Earth's bounty but are running an ecological deficit and eroding the planet's natural capital.

When we look at North America, the problem becomes more severe. North Americans have the largest ecological footprints in the world. The average American footprint is 9.6 hectares, or about twenty football fields in size (second largest in the world behind the United Arab Emirates). The average Canadian footprint of 7.6 hectares is third largest in the world, and the Australian footprint of 6.6 hectares is sixth largest. If everyone living in the world today consumed resources and produced waste at the prolific rate of North Americans and Australians, then we'd need three or four additional planets like Earth.

The average ecological footprint for a Western European is 4.8 hectares, half the size of the American footprint despite similar levels of economic prosperity. Europeans offer the rest of the world many lessons in living sustainably, including their use of extensive public transportation systems, small vehicles, and compact cities; their efficient buildings, appliances, and heating systems; their tough rules for toxic chemicals; and their strong efforts to reduce air and water pollution. But even the ecological footprints of Europeans are unsustainable and lead to significant environmental impacts (see Figures).

Despite the emergence of environmentalism as a powerful social movement, the sheer number of humans and our collective appetite for resources mean that our ecological impacts in the decades ahead could become even larger. Economic growth and an increasing human population could worsen the world's environmental problems. From this perspective, it's obvious that something must be done to reduce the ecological footprint of people living in wealthy industrialized nations. A reduction of North Americans' ecological footprint by at least 75% to less than 2 hectares per person is needed to achieve a sustainable future. This is similar to the levels of greenhouse gas reductions (60% to 80%) that scientists indicate are necessary by mid-century to avoid triggering catastrophic climate change.

## Average electricity use per capita (kilowatt hours)

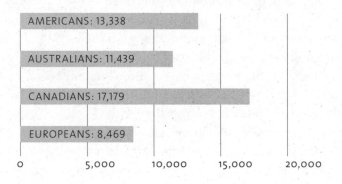

## Average water use per capita (cubic meters)

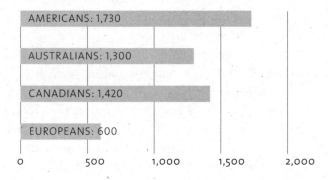

## Average amount of carbon dioxide generated by energy use per capita (metric tons)

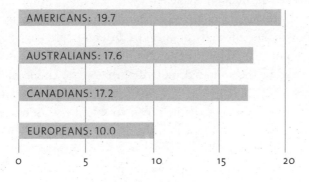

AMERICANS: 19.7
AUSTRALIANS: 17.6
CANADIANS: 17.2
EUROPEANS: 10.0

0    5    10    15    20

## Average volume of air pollution (sulfur dioxides, nitrogen oxides, volatile organic carbons, and carbon monoxide) generated per capita (kilograms)

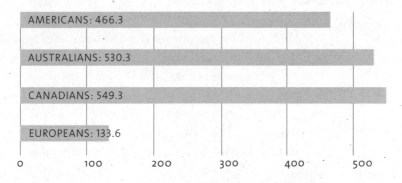

AMERICANS: 466.3
AUSTRALIANS: 530.3
CANADIANS: 549.3
EUROPEANS: 133.6

0    100    200    300    400    500

This is a defining moment in human history. With the possible exception of nuclear war, there has never been a greater threat to future generations than today's global environmental crisis. Paradoxically, there has never been a greater opportunity for profound change.

Human beings are remarkable animals. The quality that sets us apart from the vast majority of other species on Earth is our ability to think ahead, contemplate the consequences of different options, plot a course, and act accordingly. We only have to think back to 1957, when the world was electrified by the announcement that the Soviet Union had successfully launched Sputnik, the first manmade object to be hurled into space. The U.S. was galvanized to launch its own satellites, but every attempt failed in spectacular explosions on the launch pad or shortly after lift-off. The Soviets launched the first animal, a dog named Laika, the first human, Yuri Gagarin, the first team of cosmonauts, and the first woman, Valentina Tereshkova, while the U.S. struggled to get its space program up and running. No voices were raised to say America couldn't afford to compete with the U.S.S.R. or that it would destroy the economy. The North American Space Agency (NASA) was formed. Recognizing that the Soviets were advanced in math, science, engineering, and medicine, the U.S. spent massive amounts of money to support science. President John F. Kennedy made his famous assertion that the U.S. would win the race to the moon. Not only were the Americans the first country to land people on the moon, but in 2006, almost fifty years after Sputnik, Americans won every Nobel Prize in science because the U.S. took up the challenge and threw everything behind it. Today we face ecological challenges far more daunting than the space race or the cold war. We need to allocate the effort and resources for a suitably ambitious response.

By using our unique foresight, we can envision a different future, a sustainable future. After a destructive period of human arrogance, we are on the brink of an environmental revolution inspired by the wisdom and genius of nature. By patterning our economy after the natural world, which has had almost 4 billion years to work out the wrinkles, we can achieve a sustainable society that can endure and flourish for countless generations to come. In the natural world, nothing is wasted. Zero waste needs to become the basis of the human economy as well as nature's economy. The success or failure of the twenty-first century's sustainability revolution will determine the future of humankind and many species on Earth.

This is a time of transition between the industrial era and the sustainability era. We are slowly replacing an economy that ignores ecological limits with an economy that respects ecological limits. We are near the end of an era known for profligate consumption of dirty energy and at the beginning of an era where conservation, efficiency, and clean energy will predominate. Within one or two generations, humanity will rely primarily on energy that releases few or no climate-changing carbon emissions. We are moving away from being a society that recklessly uses toxic chemicals without adequate knowledge about their impacts on human health and the environment. With human ingenuity and nature's inspiration we can redesign everything we make to virtually eliminate the production and use of toxic substances. We are shifting away from being a society that consumes resources at one end and spews out waste at the other. We are becoming a society where the very idea of waste is anathema. We are evolving into a society where words like disposable, garbage, gas guzzler, and factory farm will soon be seen as anachronisms, if not obscenities. We are on our way to becoming a society that looks back on the twentieth century's excesses as a form of temporary insanity.

People's values are evolving rapidly. Five decades ago the environmental movement, as we know it, didn't exist. There was no Greenpeace, no World Wildlife Fund. Not a single country in the world had a ministry of the environment. Today, tens of millions of people belong to environmental organizations. Every government in the world has an environment department. In recent years, over seventy nations, from France to Finland and Argentina to Zambia, have amended their constitutions to recognize that all people have the right to live in a healthy and ecologically balanced environment. Constitutions in many nations now place the right to a healthy environment on par with other fundamental human rights. More than just words on paper, constitutional environmental rights will continue to have a profound influence on educating the public, tipping the balance in favor of the environment in policy decisions, and ensuring that disadvantaged groups enjoy environmental justice. Constitutional environmental rights have been central in securing clean drinking water for communities in Argentina, cleaner air in the large cities of India, and protection of biodiversity in Finland and Costa Rica.

A sustainable future lies within the reach of our imaginations. Imagine a vehicle whose only waste product is water (we're not referring to a bicycle and your sweat). Imagine getting a check from your utility company every month instead of a bill, because your home generates more electricity than it consumes. Imagine fresh, delicious, and nutritious food grown locally without pesticides, antibiotics, genetically modified organisms, or growth hormones. Imagine an agricultural system where trees, perennial grasses, cattle, chickens, and hogs are raised in sustainable, humane ways with few resources from off the farm and no waste. Imagine a city without noise and pollution from the infernal internal combustion engine. Imagine never having to worry that invisible environmental hazards are undermining your health and your children's health. Imagine industrialized nations that consume no fossil fuels, relying instead on solar energy, geothermal energy, and other sources of clean energy. Imagine that every product you buy is free from toxic chemicals, and that when things eventually wear out or break down, their manufacturer is responsible for taking care of them. Imagine that everything you ever buy is biodegradable, reusable, or recyclable.

Does this description of the future sound like a dream, or a science fiction version of ecological utopia? Perhaps, but it's not. These developments are much closer to becoming reality than many people realize, as the following examples illustrate.

Every plant on the planet derives its energy from the sun, through the process of photosynthesis. More solar energy reaches the Earth in one hour than all humans use in one year. Yet despite its immense potential, solar power is only beginning to be harnessed on a large scale for electricity generation. The largest solar photovoltaic power plant in the world is a 40-megawatt plant in Germany, the result of rapid developments since 2004—when the largest plant could generate only 6 megawatts of electricity. The growth of large solar thermal power plants—which use mirrors and lenses to concentrate the heat of the sun to extremely high temperatures—promises to be even more dramatic. While the largest single solar thermal plant in the world today is an 80-megawatt plant, much larger solar thermal facilities are being planned or constructed in California, Florida, Egypt, and South Africa. A major American utility company, Pacific Gas and Electric, recently signed a contract to buy 553 megawatts of solar power from a solar thermal facility being built in the Mojave Desert. Covering 23 square kilometers (9 square miles), the solar power plant will provide enough power for four hundred thousand homes in California, making it the largest solar power plant in the world. An even more ambitious solar thermal project is being discussed for the Sahara Desert, which could potentially provide all of the electricity needed by Europe, the Middle East, and North Africa while covering less than 0.5% of the desert.

Researchers at the University of New South Wales in Australia have made a series of breakthroughs in solar technology. They are using special titanium oxide ceramics to harvest sunlight and split water, producing hydrogen fuel. Rooftop panels placed on several million houses could meet Australia's entire electricity needs. Solar cells on metal sheets thinner than paper represent another exciting technological breakthrough. These thin-film solar cells, named 2007's innovation of the year by *Popular Science*, could be used to coat everything from buildings to cell phones, creating unprecedented energy independence.

An American company called Nanosolar is already manufacturing and selling thin-film solar cells.

## Inspiration

Sweden is pursuing a comprehensive strategy to eliminate the nation's dependence on oil by 2020. Swedish reliance on oil already dropped from 77% to 32% of total energy consumption between 1973 and 2003. The new strategy, developed by a blue-ribbon Commission on Oil Independence, includes switching vehicles to biofuels; ending the practice of heating residential and commercial buildings with oil; accelerating development of renewable energy; district heating (using co-generation and waste heat to meet domestic needs); taxes on nonrenewable energy sources, carbon emissions, and vehicle use; and grants to municipalities to invest in sustainable projects. As the Commission concluded, "We are technology optimists and want Sweden to be at the forefront in the use of new, resource-efficient, renewable technology—hybrid vehicles, solar cells, wave energy, fuel cell vehicles, new biofuels, and energy-saving IT solutions." The goal of oil independence is part of a remarkable Swedish strategy to solve all of the country's environmental problems over the course of the next generation.

Iceland aims to be the world's first hydrogen economy by 2050, using its hydroelectric and geothermal energy resources to produce hydrogen. The primary advantage of using hydrogen as a fuel is that it produces no polluting by-products at all, only clean water. Hydrogen fuel cell buses already run on the streets of Reykjavik, Iceland's capital. The world's first commercial hydrogen filling station opened on a busy downtown street in 2003. The government's goal is to convert all of Iceland's motor vehicles and the fishing fleet to hydrogen in the decades ahead.

An island called Samso off the coast of Denmark is earning global acclaim for rapidly converting from fossil fuel dependency to renewable energy. Since 1997 Samso has commissioned an offshore wind farm that produces more electricity than the island (with a population of about

4,300) consumes, has built several district heating systems that rely on solar power, straw, and wood chips to heat houses, and plans to grow canola to provide biodiesel for vehicles. In less than a decade, Samso has gone from relying on fossil fuels for 92% of its electricity and 85% of its heat to producing 100% renewable energy for both electricity and heat.

### Zero Energy Buildings

Zero energy buildings are energy-efficient buildings that rely on renewable energy, usually generated by solar panels, to produce as much energy as they consume over the course of a year. These buildings can be ordinary looking (except for the solar panels on the roof), offer healthy indoor environments, and require minimal maintenance. Zero energy buildings are already being built in the U.S., Canada, Australia, the U.K., Sweden, Germany, Portugal, and Austria. The British government recently unveiled a proposal to ensure that *all* new houses be zero energy, beginning in 2016. Ambitious architects and engineers are going even further and creating energy-plus buildings—buildings that produce more energy than they consume—in locations ranging from Austria to Thailand. An entire community of energy-plus buildings is already up and running in Freiburg, Germany, where homes are generating two or three times the amount of electricity they consume in a year.

There are already hundreds of zero energy homes in the U.S., in locations as diverse as Chicago, Illinois, Boulder, Colorado, and Salem, Oregon. The largest zero energy housing development in the U.S. is in Watsonville, California. The project includes 177 single-family homes, 80 townhomes, 132 apartments, a park, and an elementary school. Buildings feature solar panels to generate electricity, tankless solar water heaters, increased insulation, reflective roofs, tightly sealed ducts, energy-efficient appliances and windows, compact fluorescent lights, and water-saving plumbing fixtures and landscaping.

The Drake Landing Solar Community in Okotoks, Alberta, is the first housing development in North America to use district heating powered by the sun. Solar panels capture the sun's heat and store it underground to provide heat in the winter. The result will be a reduction of at least 80% in greenhouse gas emissions from this community.

The Mata de Sesimbra project being built in Portugal includes zero energy buildings, a large nature reserve, restoration of a large cork forest, a twenty-year zero waste plan, 100% renewable energy, and a pledge to get 50% of food in onsite stores and restaurants from local growers and producers.

### Zero Emission Vehicles

Zero emission vehicles are already being manufactured, albeit in small quantities and at high prices. Prototype hydrogen fuel cell vehicles are already operating on city streets in Vancouver, Chicago, and many European cities. Quantum Technologies is already delivering hydrogen fueled Toyota Priuses to Norway. Fully electric vehicles with limited range and speed—from companies including Xebra, ZENN, and Miles Automotive—are already available at car dealers. Increasingly sophisticated zero emission electric vehicles such as the Aptera are generating buzz at auto shows around the world. For example, the Tesla Roadster is a fully electric vehicle that can go from 0 to 100 kilometers (60 miles) per hour in four seconds, has a range of 390 kilometers (245 miles), and is expected to go into production in 2008. Phoenix Motorcars is selling full-function electric pickup trucks that can travel more than 160 kilometers (100 miles) on a charge.

### Zero Waste

Zero waste is catching on as a goal for individuals, corporations, and municipal governments. Zero waste means redesigning patterns of production and consumption to ensure that everything used or produced is reusable, recyclable, or safely biodegradable. The benefits of zero waste include job creation and economic development, reduced waste disposal costs, and reduced greenhouse gas emissions. In New Zealand, nearly three-quarters of local governments have passed resolutions setting zero waste as a goal, and some areas have already reduced the amount of waste going to landfills by up to 90%. New Zealand was the first country in the world to recognize that women have the right to vote, the first country to have a national nuclear-free policy, and is striving to become the first waste-free country.

## Sustainable Agriculture

Sustainable agriculture is making a comeback. Sales of local and organic food are skyrocketing. Farmers and scientists in the U.S. are reimagining the production of food, using natural models for inspiration. Wes Jackson and the Land Institute are striving to emulate native prairies, enabling farmers to harvest a diversity of grain crops without annual plantings. This visionary approach aims to improve the security of food systems by decreasing dependency upon fossil fuels, reducing soil erosion, and alleviating the chemical contamination of land and water by pesticides. As Jackson writes, "The wild prairie, unlike current agriculture, holds soil, provides its own fertility, runs on sunlight, efficiently manages rainfall, and is not plagued by weeds or epidemics of pests or diseases. We can fashion an agriculture with the same benefits." Many farmers, including Joel Salatin and his Polyface Farm, are recreating the natural cycle whereby the land nourishes animals, and animals nourish the land.

## Sustainable Products

Makers of seemingly mundane products—including underwear, carpets, shoes, and office furniture—are applying a radical new design philosophy called the cradle-to-cradle approach. Developed by chemist Michael Braungart and architect William McDonough, the concept is breathtakingly simple. Everything we make and use must be capable of entering one of two streams at the end of its useful life: the biological stream or the technological stream. The biological stream involves returning biodegradable materials to the land, enriching the soil so that we can grow more food, forests, fibers, and flowers. The technological stream requires materials to be endlessly cycled, manufactured over and over again. In McDonough's words, "The materials go back to soils safely, or they go back to industry. That's it. That's the new paradigm." The cradle-to-cradle approach is making the leap from vision to reality. McDonough and Braungart have awarded cradle-to-cradle certification for meeting their rigorous sustainability criteria to dozens of innovative products, including fabrics, all-purpose cleaners, diapers, building exteriors, wall coverings, and surfboard wax.

Interface Carpets, a U.S. company led by sustainability champion Ray Anderson, is a major manufacturer that employs the cradle-to-cradle approach. Interface's ambitious goal, Mission Zero, is to eliminate the company's negative impacts on the environment by 2020. Interface invented a glueless installation process (no more toxic volatile organic compounds), designed a line of completely biodegradable carpets, eliminated the use of heavy metals, and recycled over 45 million kilograms (100 million pounds) of carpet that would otherwise have ended up in landfill sites. Over the course of a decade, waste is down 70%, energy use down 50%, greenhouse gas emissions down 60%, and water use down 80%. In addition to these environmental benefits, Interface saved over $300 million, enjoyed record sales levels, and saw share prices soar. Shaw Industries, another large carpet manufacturer, also offers carpets that can be recycled over and over into new carpet, not recycled into inferior products or dumped in landfills. Shaw's sustainable carpet also cut manufacturing costs by more than 10%.

Steelcase and Herman Miller, large office equipment manufacturers, are committed to refurbishing or recycling all office products that they manufacture and have developed a line of upholstery fabrics that, unlike conventional fabrics containing toxic substances, are safely biodegradable.

Patagonia, a leading maker of outdoor clothing, operates the Common Threads Garment Recycling Program, which encourages customers to return their worn-out clothing—polyester fleece, organic cotton t-shirts, and polyester underwear—to the company. The used clothing is used to remanufacture new garments. The program reduces waste by diverting used clothing from landfills, reduces energy use by 76%, and cuts greenhouse gas emissions by 71%. Canada's Mountain Equipment Co-op recently started a similar program.

Even Nike, once reviled by activists, has adopted the principles of cradle-to-cradle design. Nike's environmental policy strives for zero toxics, zero waste, and 100% recovery, recycling, and reuse of the products they manufacture. Nike recently released a basketball shoe called TrashTalk made entirely from scrap materials and is designing a running shoe with a biodegradable sole and an upper portion that can be endlessly remanufactured into new shoes.

The resource savings, elimination of waste, and reduced environmental pressure embodied in the cradle-to-cradle approach are essential to the future of humankind when you envision a future of 9 billion people seeking a high standard of living.

### WHAT CAN YOU DO?

The seeds of a sustainable future are germinating but need to be carefully nurtured. Unfortunately, we don't yet live in a world where all of our options are sustainable choices. Coal and gas-fired power plants still dwarf solar power, wind power, and other zero emission sources of electricity. Only a handful of zero energy housing developments exist. We can't yet visit a local car dealer and choose between electric cars and hydrogen fuel cell vehicles. Local and organically grown foods make up a minority of overall food consumption. Toxic chemicals are still used in myriad consumer products, while cradle-to-cradle products constitute a tiny fraction of industrial output.

We can't afford to wait for future technological advances to save the biosphere. Although our individual actions may seem trivial, they are not. The effect of one person bringing his or her own bag to the supermarket may seem inconsequential in the global context, a tiny drop in the bucket. But if we all brought our own bags, the total impact would be enormous, in the same way that enough drops can fill a bucket. The same logic applies to actions like switching to compact fluorescent light bulbs. When one person or a few dedicated environmentalists do it, the effects are negligible. But when an entire community, state, or nation makes the switch, as Canada and Australia are proposing, the impact can be enormous. Planned coal-fired generating plants can be taken off the drawing board. Nuclear plants can be mothballed. Until the sustainability revolution arrives in full force, we need to buy some time for the beleaguered planet. That's why we need to do everything we can to reduce our ecological footprints today. No one sets out to deliberately ruin the planet, but to varying degrees we are all part of the problem. In so many ways, through ignorance, laziness, or indifference, our actions add up to a destructive effect. Once we become aware of the impact humanity is having, the challenge is to deliberately change deeply engrained habits.

This book identifies the individual actions that cause the most environmental damage and describes the most effective ways to reduce your impact. The three areas of individual or family action that have the greatest environmental impacts are related to household activities (heating, cooling, appliance use, lighting, etc.), food, and transport. Together these three areas represent roughly 80% of the average North American's contribution to climate change, air pollution, water pollution, and the loss of biodiversity.

Chapters 2, 3, and 4 are dedicated to exploring green choices in each of these areas:
· The homes where we live.
· The food we eat.
· The way we travel.

Chapter 5 describes how to make greener choices for all of the other stuff we buy. And while actions by committed individuals can put a dent in the global environmental crisis, they cannot solve it, so Chapter 6 identifies how you can exercise your democratic powers to promote policies that ensure everyone—citizens, politicians, bureaucrats, and business people—behaves in a sustainable way. Laws, taxes, subsidies, and policies of all kinds need to be transformed in order to accelerate the sustainability revolution. As Al Gore says, "changing light bulbs is useful, but it's more important to change laws." Economic policies need to be rewritten to incorporate ecological reality. Subsidies that encourage environmentally destructive behavior need to be terminated. Taxes need to be shifted away from activities that society wants to encourage, like employment and investment, onto activities that society seeks to discourage, like waste, pollution, and the use of toxic chemicals. Governments need to measure progress more holistically, rediscover the effectiveness of strong environmental regulations, and allocate far more resources to promoting environmental solutions. None of these policy changes is likely to be implemented without sustained pressure from concerned citizens.

By following the advice in this book, you won't suffer a loss in the quality of your life but you will:

· Generate fewer climate-changing greenhouse gas emissions.
· Produce less water pollution.
· Cause less air pollution.
· Discard less waste.
· Use up fewer natural resources.
· Reduce your exposure to toxic chemicals.
· Relieve pressure on endangered species and their habitat.

Following our recommendations will enable you to reduce your ecological footprint to half or even as little as one-tenth of its current size. This may sound impossible but consider the dramatic effects of these everyday examples of technological and behavioral change:

· Today's most energy-efficient refrigerators use less than one-quarter of the energy of refrigerators made a generation ago (and no longer use the chemicals that were destroying the Earth's irreplaceable ozone layer).
· Recycled aluminum cans use just 5% of the energy required to make aluminum cans from virgin materials.

- A laptop computer uses as little as one-tenth the energy that a desktop computer uses.
- Printing on both sides of paper reduces paper consumption by 50%.

Kermit the frog was wrong when he said "it ain't easy being green." The actions outlined in this book don't require sacrifices. You don't have to switch to a raw food diet, or trade in your comfortable home for a tent or a cave. We're not physically addicted to stuff. There are no painful withdrawal symptoms when we change our consumption habits. To the contrary, in addition to reducing your contribution to global environmental problems, you'll also:

- Improve your health.
- Save money.
- Feel less guilty and less helpless.
- Enhance your quality of life.

Perhaps most importantly, reducing your ecological footprint is likely to make you happier. Materialistic values actually undermine our well-being by perpetuating feelings of insecurity and by weakening the ties that bind us to families, friends, and communities. Individuals with materialistic values are more likely to suffer anxiety and depression, watch more television, abuse alcohol and drugs, and have unsatisfying personal relationships. In contrast, people who ride bicycles, recycle, and appreciate nature tend to be happier, healthier, and more fulfilled.

There are millions of people doing their best to achieve a sustainable, just, and prosperous future. Every reduction in the size of your ecological footprint takes a little bit of pressure off the planet. We are in trouble. The Earth is warning us that we must change course, and there's no time to waste. Join the sustainability revolution!

# 2

# Home Smart Home

*We shape our buildings*
*and afterwards our buildings shape us.*
WINSTON CHURCHILL

❦ ❦ ❦

Gas-guzzling SUVs get a lot of blame for creating pollution and causing climate change, and rightly so. But the average home in North
America and other parts of the industrialized world actually causes
more than twice the greenhouse gas emissions of the average vehicle.
Part of the problem is that when we flip a switch or turn on a tap, the
environmental consequences are out of sight and out of mind. Electricity and water appear to be limitless and using them in vast quantities
seems benign. The reality is that building and living in today's homes
accounts for 70% of electricity use, 35% of greenhouse gas emissions, and
approximately 30% of landfill waste in the U.S. and Canada. The total
footprint of an average single-family house includes over 300 metric tons
(660,000 pounds) of material, and is growing. In the U.S., the size of a
new house increased by at least 45 meters (500 square feet) every twenty
years between 1950 and 1990 (see Table 2). Yet average household size in
the U.S. has fallen from 3.3 people to 2.6 people since 1960 and the trend
in other parts of the industrialized world is similar. Bigger houses plus
smaller households equals environmental trouble.

TABLE 2. *Average size of new homes in the U.S. (square meters)*

| 1950 | 90 (1,000 sq. ft.) |
|------|--------------------|
| 1970 | 135 (1,500 sq. ft.) |
| 1990 | 187 (2,080 sq. ft.) |
| 2005 | 219 (2,434 sq. ft.) |

As immense as the volume of materials involved in the construction of a new home may seem, they comprise a small fraction of the total ecological footprint of a home over its lifespan. In other words, the impacts of living in a home, mostly energy use, are far greater than the impacts of construction and demolition. Detached single-family residences use the most energy and are the most common form of housing in many wealthy industrialized nations. Compared with a detached single-family home on a large lot, a house on a small lot has a footprint that is 8% smaller, a townhouse has a footprint that is 22% smaller, and an apartment in a high-rise has a footprint that is 40% smaller. When it comes to housing, small is beautiful—smaller homes require less material and energy to build, maintain, and operate (and have less room for accumulating junk!).

## WHAT YOU CAN DO

Buildings last much longer than most industrial products. Only a small proportion—1% or 2%—of the total housing stock is built new each year. As a result, the total environmental impact of new buildings is dwarfed by existing buildings. While we must move as quickly as possible to make zero energy homes the standard for new construction, as the U.K. is doing, we also need to dramatically improve the performance of existing homes.

There are four important steps you can take to reduce the ecological footprint associated with where you live:

1. Choosing a modest-sized home near work, school, recreation, and public transit.

2. Getting a home energy audit and following the recommendations.
3. Buying green electricity.
4. Finding ways to use energy and water more efficiently.

## LOCATION, LOCATION, LOCATION

Perhaps the single most important determinant of your ecological footprint is your home's location. Living in detached homes in distant suburbs causes higher home energy use, higher transportation costs (in terms of time, money, and pollution), and higher infrastructure costs. Next time you move, look for a comfortable yet modest home in an area where you can use your car less. Look for a neighborhood with safe streets for walking, cycling, and children, lots of trees, and proximity to attractive green spaces. Choosing to live close to where you work, study, and play, and living in a reasonably sized home can have a tremendous effect on your ecological footprint and is likely to increase your happiness and quality of life.

## SAVE ENERGY, SAVE MONEY, SAVE THE PLANET

*Conservation means freezing in the dark.*—RONALD REAGAN

Reagan was wrong. Conservation actually means living comfortably at a small portion of the cost of our wasteful lifestyles. Every time you turn on the television, take a shower, buy a new appliance, or replace a burned-out light bulb, you're making a decision that affects the environment. You already know that using energy contributes to climate change, smog, oil spills, and acid rain. But you may not realize just how big a difference you can make by taking energy use into account in your daily activities and household purchasing decisions.

In order to identify your energy-saving priorities, you need to identify the biggest contributors to your home's ecological footprint. To some extent this will depend on the climate where you live, your utility's energy supply, your energy use patterns, and home size and features. For instance, electricity in Canada tends to be much cleaner than in the U.S., because burning coal, natural gas, and oil generates almost three-quarters of American electricity but only one-quarter of Canadian electricity. In some parts of the world, your electricity may come from hydropower, which makes a minimal contribution to climate change. In most American states and many other places, however, the lion's share of electricity comes from burning coal or natural gas—activities that emit huge quantities of climate-changing carbon dioxide.

Our advice is based on average North American energy use, but no matter where you live in the world, using energy more wisely will save money, protect the environment, and make your home a healthier, more comfortable place.

The cost of using energy in American and Canadian homes averages almost $2,000 per year, with heating requiring the most energy, followed by operating appliances, heating hot water, and lighting (see Table 3). Between 1978 and 2001, the total amount of energy used by Americans for heating fell by 30%, despite a significant increase in the number of homes. Similar progress has been made in Canada. The gains were due to more efficient building techniques, weatherizing older homes, and perhaps the warmer weather associated with climate change. Despite these advances, there's still ample room for improvement. In the U.S., only 40% of residences are well insulated, and less than 40% of new windows sold are energy efficient.

Your home is your castle, but it doesn't have to feel like one. No sane person would leave a door open on a cold winter day, yet many houses leak so much air through gaps and cracks that this is effectively what people are doing. Heat escapes in the winter and invades in the summer. Furnaces and air conditioners are forced to work harder than necessary, increasing the risk of breakdown and shortening their lifespan. These inadequacies waste energy, waste money, and reduce your level of comfort, yet can be remedied.

Every step you take to reduce electricity use in your home has up to three times the impact that you might imagine. This is because of a phenomenon called energy conversion loss. Losses occur during the generation, transmission, and distribution of electricity. For every unit of electricity that you use in your home, as many as three units of primary energy are consumed by the power system. Keep this important fact in mind if you have doubts about whether your actions make a significant difference.

For many investments in energy efficiency, you'll receive a very good return on your investment. The term payback period describes the time it takes to recoup your investment in enhanced efficiency through lower energy costs. If you spend $25 on an insulating jacket for your hot water heater and your utility bill drops by $5 a month, the payback period is five months. On top of lower utility bills, there's more good financial news if you own your home. For every dollar cut from utility bills through conservation and efficiency, the value of a home rises by $20. Lower your annual utility bill by $500 and your house gains $10,000 in value. Increased energy efficiency is also a form of insurance against rising energy prices.

TABLE 3. *Major uses of energy in homes in some industrialized countries*

| HOME ENERGY USE | AUSTRALIA | CANADA | U.K. | U.S. |
|---|---|---|---|---|
| Space heating/cooling | 39% | 57% | 60% | 49% |
| Appliances and electronics | 29% | 13% | 14% | 20% |
| Water heating | 27% | 24% | 23% | 15% |
| Lighting | 5% | 5% | 3% | 7% |

### GET AN ENERGY AUDIT

The best way to get accurate advice on the most effective and economical steps you can take to upgrade your home's energy performance is to get a professional energy audit. This is like having a doctor perform a complete physical exam to provide you with a personalized strategy for improving your health. Although every home is built and maintained differently, energy audits generally focus on four key areas: airtightness, insulation, windows, and heating and cooling systems. Further information on locating a home energy auditor (also called a home performance analyst) is available from government websites (e.g., www.energystar.gov in the U.S.; www.ecoaction.gc.ca in Canada; www.energyconservation.com.au in Australia; www.energysavingtrust.org.uk in the United Kingdom). In some jurisdictions, an energy audit makes you eligible for government rebates when you improve your home's energy efficiency. But even without a grant, you'll recoup your investment quickly by following the advice provided by an energy audit. If you can't afford a professional audit, helpful Internet sites for evaluating your home's energy use by yourself are available. In Australia, see www.yourhome.gov.au. In Canada, see www.powerwise.ca. In the U.K., see www.resurgence.org/energy/neac/index.htm. In the U.S., see http://hes.lbl.gov/hes/db/zip.shtml.

## Make Your Home Airtight

Energy audits will identify cracks, crevices, and holes in the walls, attic, and floors. Plugging these leaks will reduce heating and cooling costs by 5% to 30%. Weather stripping and caulking around windows and doors is usually a great investment, saving an average of $1.54 per dollar invested. Additional benefits of airtightness include improved comfort, especially during hot or cold weather, a quieter home because less noise enters from the outside, fewer holes where pollen, dust, pollution, and insects can enter your home, and improved durability. While making your home airtight it is essential to maintain adequate ventilation in order to avoid indoor air quality problems.

## Add Insulation

Only 20% of homes built before 1980 have adequate insulation. Think about trying to stay warm on a cold and windy winter day. You need both a warm jacket (insulation) and a windbreaker (a vapor barrier). The effectiveness of insulation is measured by its R-value. The higher the R-value, the more effective the insulation. Eco-friendly insulation options include products made from cellulose (recycled wood or paper) and recycled denim.

## Upgrade Heating and Cooling Systems

In some countries, such as Canada and the U.S., home heating is dominated by wasteful systems, with low- and medium-efficiency furnaces
outnumbering high-efficiency furnaces. The following suggestions will
cut the energy needed to heat your home while maintaining or even
improving comfort levels, and in some cases saving money:

· Replace an older heating system with an energy-efficient furnace,
  which will be at least 20% more efficient.
· Check and replace filters regularly, get an annual tune-up, and make
  sure all ducts are properly sealed to ensure maximum airflow.
· Install a programmable thermostat to save 5% to 10% on your energy bill.
· If you live in the northern hemisphere, plant coniferous trees on the
  north side of your home to block cold winds and deciduous trees on the
  south side to provide summer shade. Wherever you live, carefully posi-
  tioned trees can save up to 25% of the energy a typical household uses
  for cooling.
· Use fans as an effective and economical substitute for air conditioning.
  On average, a ceiling fan will use only about one-tenth of the electricity
  per year that an air conditioner uses.
· If you have an ample budget, consider a green roof. Roofs specially
  designed to be covered by soil and plants are a more ambitious way to
  cut energy use for heating and cooling while offering additional benefits by providing wildlife habitat and reducing runoff.

In addition, you might want to consider the following no-cost tips for
reducing energy from heating and cooling:

· Close curtains or blinds at night during the winter and during the
  day in summer.
· Turn the thermostat down by 1 or 2 degrees.
· Turn the thermostat way down while you're away at work or on
  vacation.

### Replace Old Windows

Windows cost the U.S. 2 million barrels of oil per day in wasted energy. The good news is that today's high-quality windows are six times more energy efficient than older windows. Because new windows are expensive, they may not be the top priority in improving your home's energy efficiency. However, new windows also offer improved comfort, aesthetics, and resale value. Windows are rated according to their U-value. The lower the U-value, the better the window. Choose energy-efficient windows that are certified to outperform regular windows, and are designed for maximum performance in your specific climate zone.

### Inspiration

Carbon Busters Inc. is a consulting firm that advises school boards, municipalities, and businesses about using energy more efficiently. So far, Carbon Busters' advice has reduced carbon dioxide emissions by 54 million kilograms (121 million pounds), yet this huge environmental improvement cost the clients nothing. Carbon Busters was paid a portion of the savings on energy costs, while the clients themselves saved more than $16 million.

### Buy Energy-efficient Appliances and Electronics

Large appliances that were once energy guzzlers have gone on a diet thanks to efficiency regulations. Compared with 1990 models, an average new fridge today uses 50% less electricity, a freezer 48% less, a dishwasher 65% less, a clothes washer 53% less, a dryer 17% less, and a range 15% less. The opposite holds true for the myriad other appliances, electronics, and gadgets that are becoming ubiquitous—coffee machines, iPods, DVD players, cell phones, cordless phones, computers, digital cameras, electric toothbrushes, and so on. In Canada, energy consumption by these products jumped 71% between 1990 and 2004. Worldwide, people own billions of electronic items that rely on rechargeable batteries. The majority of the energy consumed by these rechargeable items occurs when the batteries are already full but still in the charger, or when the charger is plugged in without batteries.

Our advice regarding appliances and electronics is simple: buy the most efficient model that is able to meet your needs. Avoid fancy gizmos like water and ice dispensers on fridges, as they suck up extra energy. At a minimum, purchase products certified as energy efficient. There are Energy Star program choices in numerous categories of consumer products, including residential appliances, heating, ventilating and air conditioning equipment, consumer electronics, office equipment, lighting, windows, and new homes. Some examples of these energy-efficient North American products can be found at www.energystar.gov and www.energystar.gc.ca. For U.K. products, visit www.energysavingtrust.org.uk. For Australian products, visit www.energystar.gov.au and www.energyrating.gov.au. In Europe, the EU Energy Label (A, A+, or A++) on all appliances helps you pick the most efficient product and the Energy Star ratings (www.eu-energystar.org) are being used more often.

You might be discouraged to learn that the price of highly efficient models is higher than less efficient products. Don't be fooled by this misleading comparison! It makes more sense (economically and environmentally) to consider the total life cycle costs of products, including energy costs. From this perspective, the most efficient model is generally cheaper, despite its higher initial price. For example, compare a front-loading washer that uses 275 kilowatt hours per year with a top-loading washer that uses 827 kwh. The energy-efficient model might cost an extra $100, but over its fifteen-year lifespan it could save you $825 in energy costs (plus further savings on water). Although energy-efficient products offer better quality and lower total costs, most people still don't get it. For instance, only one in three fridges purchased in the U.S. and Canada today is an energy-efficient model.

As well as buying more efficient appliances and electronics, consider the following no-cost tips for saving energy and money:

- Dry your washing on a clothesline or rack.
- Keep fridge and oven doors closed as much as possible.
- Use small appliances such as a microwave or toaster oven for cooking instead of the range.
- Defrost food in the fridge, not in the microwave and not under running hot water.
- Use pots and pans with tight-fitting lids and match them to the size of the burner.
- Clean the lint trap before using the dryer.
- Do full loads in the clothes washer and dishwasher, and use the economy setting.
- Use cold water whenever possible in the washing machine—most of the energy consumed by washing clothes is used to heat water, not run the machine.
- Use a laptop computer and activate its sleep mode.
- Turn your computer off when not using it. This will not harm it. Screen savers do not, contrary to popular belief, save energy.

## Turn It Off!

You can use appliances and electronics much more efficiently. Few people realize that many electronic items consume electricity even when they're turned off or not in use. Classic examples include cordless phones, all kinds of battery rechargers, televisions, and microwave ovens. This is called the phantom load, and it's like a leaky faucet except you can't see the wasted electricity. Up to 75% of the electricity used by home electronics is consumed while the products are turned off. The easiest way to reduce or eliminate this wasted energy is to plug these items into a power bar, or power strip, and turn the bar off when the items are not in use.

## Recycle Old Appliances

Old fridges lurking in basements or garages are probably electricity hogs. In Canada, more than one in three households has two refrigerators. Some utilities in Canada and the U.S. will pick up your old fridge, recycle it, reduce your electricity bill by about $100 per year, and as an added incentive, send you a check. In Europe, retailers now have an obligation to take back old electric appliances (including fridges) when you buy a new product, no matter where you bought the original appliance.

### Inspiration

When energy efficiency standards for household appliances were proposed back in the 1970s, manufacturers balked, claiming that better technology either didn't exist or would send appliance costs skyrocketing. They were wrong. The net benefit to consumers from energy efficiency standards for appliances in the U.S. between 1987 and 2030 will be $130 billion. Greenhouse gas emissions will be reduced by almost 1 billion tons of carbon dioxide in total over this period. In 2006 alone, energy-efficient products purchased in the U.S. reduced electricity use by 170 billion kilowatt hours, saving American consumers $14 billion on their utility bills. Similarly, Canada is expected to reduce annual carbon dioxide emissions by 26 million tons by 2010 thanks to energy efficiency regulations. These regulations will have an effect equivalent to taking 4 million cars off the road.

### Water Heating

You'd never think of leaving your television on twenty-four hours a day just in case you decided to watch it. Yet this is exactly what we do with hot water in our homes. Your water heater constantly keeps the water hot, regardless of whether you're at home or away, awake or asleep. For most households, the energy used to heat water can be reduced by up to 50%, saving up to $200 per year. One obvious step is to use less hot water. We'll talk about actions you can take to reduce water use later in this chapter. For now, let's focus on other ways to save energy when heating water.

The cheapest and easiest way is to turn down the temperature on your hot water tank. This involves three steps for an electric water heater and just one step for a gas water heater. If you have an electric heater, first turn off the power going to the hot water tank (flip the appropriate circuit breaker in your fuse box). Second, remove the heating element access cover(s) on the side of the tank. Third, use a screwdriver to turn down the temperature on the thermostat to between 43 and 49 degrees Celsius (110 and 120 degrees Fahrenheit). If you have a gas system, just turn down the thermostat (no need to turn off the gas first). This will save energy, save money, decrease corrosion so that your heater lasts longer, and reduce the risk of scalding, especially if there are young children in the house.

Another simple way to save energy is to get insulated padding for your tank and the hot water pipes. Insulating kits can be purchased at home supply and hardware stores and will save enough energy to pay back their costs in about a year. When it's time to replace your hot water heater, buy the most efficient model available and also install a heat trap (costs less than $5) on your hot water pipes to stop cool water from circulating back into the tank.

More ambitious options for saving energy include:
· Using the sun's energy to heat your water.
· Replacing your hot water tank with an instant or tankless water heater.
· Installing a heat pump water heater.
· Using a drainwater waste heat recovery system.

Solar thermal hot water heating is an economical and environmentally friendly option in many parts of the world, even on cloudy days. More than 1.5 million homes and businesses in the U.S. have solar thermal water heating systems, and more than 94% of these customers consider the systems a good investment. A solar water heater will save about $350 per year compared with an electric water heater. During a twenty-year period, a solar water heater can eliminate more than 50 tons of carbon dioxide emissions. A useful source of independent ratings of solar water heaters is www.solar-rating.org.

Tankless or instant water heaters do not contain a storage tank. Instead, a gas burner or electric element rapidly heats water only when it is needed. Hot water never runs out, but the flow rate (amount of hot water per minute) is limited and electricity demand is high for short periods. Tankless heaters won't suit everyone, especially larger households that may require hot water for two uses at once. Heat pump water heaters use about half as much electricity as conventional electric water heaters and are most cost effective in warm climates and in homes with high water use. A drainwater waste heat recovery system, which captures the heat from used hot water and warms unused water, provides energy savings of 25% to 30%.

## Lighting

We still use nineteenth-century technology to light our homes. Less than 10% of the energy consumed by an incandescent bulb produces light while the remainder generates heat. In the U.S., lighting uses more energy than air conditioning and consumes as much electricity as all 104 American nuclear power plants produce. Because of the wastefulness of incandescent lights, Canada and Australia are planning to restrict sales beginning in 2012.

Compact fluorescent lights (CFLs), light-emitting diodes (LEDs), and halogen lights are superior options. Halogen lights are more durable and efficient than ordinary incandescent lights, although not to the same extent as CFLs and LEDs. Today's fluorescent lights have overcome past weaknesses. CFLs use one-quarter of the energy of incandescent lights, last up to ten times longer, and fit almost all conventional light fixtures. There's been a surge of interest in CFLs and sales are soaring. If every home in the U.S. replaced their five most frequently used light fixtures with CFLs, Americans would save close to $8 billion each year in energy costs, and prevent the emission of greenhouse gases equivalent to nearly 10 million cars (Table 4).

CFLs contain a very small amount of the hazardous heavy metal mercury. However, using CFLs reduces electricity use, thus reducing mercury emissions from coal-burning power plants—the largest human-

**TABLE 4.** *How much money will you save with CFLs?*

| OPERATING DETAILS | INCANDESCENT | CFL |
|---|---|---|
| Typical cost of bulb | $0.40 | $2.60 |
| Average life in hours | 1,000 | 10,000 |
| Average cost of electricity ($/kwh) | $0.10 | $0.10 |
| Power use in watts | 60 | 15 |
| Cost to operate for 10,000 hours | $60.00 | $15.00 |
| Life cycle cost (purchase price plus electricity) | $64.00 | $17.60 |
| TOTAL SAVINGS PER CFL BULB: | $46.40 | |

caused source of mercury emissions in many parts of the world. Since even a very small amount of mercury can be a health and environmental hazard, it's essential that you recycle your CFL bulbs. A growing number of retailers, led by Ikea, offer recycling programs.

LEDs are rapidly evolving and already offer an excellent choice for some lighting uses. Many cities have replaced conventional traffic lights with LEDs, which are brighter and more visible than incandescent lights, especially in direct sunlight and inclement weather. Because LEDs turn on and off instantly, signal changes are easier to see. LEDs are extremely efficient, reducing energy use by up to 90%, and durable, lasting as long as one hundred thousand hours. Work crews only have to replace them every few years, instead of every few months, adding labor savings to the energy savings. Vancouver, B.C., saves $350,000 annually because it replaced all of its incandescent traffic lights with LEDs.

One way to reduce your electricity bill and your ecological footprint is to get into the habit of turning off the lights when you leave a room. Another good habit is to clean your light fixtures regularly so that you get the maximum amount of the light they produce. When renovating, increase natural light by adding windows, skylights, or solar tubes (www. solatube.com).

For fast payback, try some of the following energy-efficient upgrades:
- Replace incandescent lights with compact fluorescent lights.
- Seal furnace ducts.
- Replace your clothes washer.
- Add a programmable thermostat.
- Wrap your water heater with an insulated blanket.
- Replace your fridge.
- Install a heat pump.
- Replace your dishwasher.
- Add weather stripping and caulking to your doors and windows.
- Add insulation.

### BUY GREEN ELECTRICITY

Once you've reduced energy use in your home, it's time to switch to 100% renewable energy. This no longer means going off the grid, growing long hair, and spending thousands of dollars to become energy self-sufficient. Instead, you can take one of two simple steps.

In a growing number of jurisdictions, you can purchase green power from your local utility. Participating customers voluntarily pay a premium on their electric bills to support renewable energy such as solar and wind power. The U.S. Environmental Protection Agency offers a handy Green Power Locator that identifies where you can buy green energy (www.epa.gov/greenpower/locator/index.htm). In Canada, you can contact your local utility or check the list compiled by the Canadian Wind Energy Association (www.canwea.ca/Green_Power_Marketing.cfm). You can also find out about green power in Australia (www.greenpower.gov.au) and the U.K. (www.eugenestandard.org).

If green power isn't available in your region yet, you can buy renewable energy certificates, also called green tags or green certificates. Renewable energy certificates enable you to support the renewable energy projects of other utility companies.

## SAVE WATER, SAVE MONEY, SAVE THE PLANET

*Water not consumed can save a river from a dam
and wetlands from destruction, while water not heated with fossil fuel
means oil or gas not depleted, coal not burned, carbon not
released to cause global warming, and sulfur not deposited as acid rain.*
—ROCKY MOUNTAIN INSTITUTE

Nobody in the world wastes more water than Americans, and Canadians are right behind. The average American uses the equivalent of 1,600 glasses of water daily (380 liters or 84 gallons), while Canadians use the equivalent of about 1,400 glasses of water daily (340 liters or 75 gallons). That's double the European average, and triple the average of nations that are leaders in using water wisely (e.g., Belgium, Germany, Denmark, and the Netherlands). Part of the problem is that water in many nations is too cheap. Most households in Canada and the U.S. pay $1 to $2 for a thousand liters of water. In other words, North Americans pay more for a can of pop, a beer, a cup of coffee, or a liter of bottled water than they pay for a thousand liters of municipally treated drinking water.

It's worth pointing out that in North America households account for less than 5% of total water use. Hydroelectric facilities, fossil fuel and nuclear power plants (which use vast amounts of water for cooling), and agriculture are the largest users. All water users in Canada and the U.S. need to conserve water because at least 36 states anticipate local, regional, or statewide water shortages by 2013, while one in four Canadian municipalities experienced a water shortage in the past five years, and climate change is expected to make things worse. In Australia, the agriculture industry accounts for almost 70% of water consumption, while households account for 11%. A severe and extended drought has led to restrictions and extensive efforts to use water more sustainably. In recent years, parts of Europe have experienced unprecedented water shortages, leading to forest fires, lower production of hydroelectricity, and water rationing.

When it comes to wasting water, the main culprits are inefficient toilets, leaking faucets, water-guzzling appliances, and thirsty lawns (see

Table 5). By following the three rules of water conservation—reduce, repair, and replace—you can slash water consumption by 50% or more and save money, with no negative effect on your lifestyle.

The average household spends about $500 per year on its water and sewer bill. By making just a few simple changes, you could save up to $250 per year. The average home, retrofitted with water-efficient fixtures, can save 135,000 liters (30,000 gallons) per year. If all U.S. households installed water-efficient fixtures and appliances, Americans could save more than 13 trillion liters of water and more than $17 billion dollars per year! If all Australians chose more water-efficient products, they could save 610 billion liters of water and $600 million by 2020. As well, using less water throughout the world would reduce the need for costly water supply and wastewater treatment infrastructure.

TABLE 5. *Indoor water use in some industrialized countries (percentage of total daily use)*

|  | AUSTRALIA | CANADA | U.K. | U.S. |
|---|---|---|---|---|
| Toilet | 27% | 30% | 35% | 27% |
| Shower and bath | 36% | 35% | 20% | 19% |
| Clothes washer | 22% | 20% | 14% | 22% |
| Cooking, drinking, cleaning | 15% | 15% | 29% | 19% |
| Leaks | No data | No data | 2% | 13% |

*Reduce*

A running tap uses about 8 liters (2 gallons) of water per minute. Reducing your water use can be achieved by cultivating a few good habits:

· Turn off the tap while you brush your teeth, wash dishes, or shave.
· Take shorter showers and save baths for special occasions.
· Use a bucket and a sponge to wash your car and a broom to clean the driveway instead of the hose.
· Keep a jug of drinking water in the refrigerator instead of letting the faucet run until the water is cold.

- Scrape rather than rinse dishes before loading them into the dishwasher.
- Wash fruits and vegetables in a basin.
- Don't use running water to defrost frozen foods (thaw in the refrigerator overnight).
- Don't pour water down the drain if you can use it for other projects like watering plants or cleaning.
- Use the economy setting on clothes washers and dishwashers.

A typical suburban lawn may need up to 100,000 liters (22,000 gallons) of water annually over and above rainfall. Think about native trees, shrubs, and flowers in your area—none of them require watering. There are no sprinklers in forests or meadows.

Ways to save water outdoors include:

- Rip out all or part of your lawn, and replace it with a vegetable garden, native plants, fruit trees, shade trees, or wildflowers.
- Practice xeriscaping, a form of landscaping that relies predominantly on rainfall, even in dry climates.
- Use mulch (a natural barrier of shredded leaves, straw, or bark) to retain moisture.

## FAQS

*Bath or shower?* It depends. A full bathtub requires 158 to 315 liters (35 to 70 gallons) of water, while a five-minute shower with a low-flow showerhead uses 45 to 68 liters.

*Dishwasher or wash by hand?* It depends. Washing the dishes with the tap running can use up to 135 liters (30 gallons) of water, but filling a basin can save 113 of those liters. The average dishwasher uses about 65 liters (15 gallons), while new models may use as few as 13 liters.

As an added bonus, getting rid of lawns also eliminates the need for polluting lawnmowers. If you're wedded to your lawn and not ready for a divorce, try these tips:

- Plant a hardy variety of grass that needs less water.
- Water early in the morning or late in the evening to avoid excessive evaporation.
- Don't overwater (once every four or five days in the summer is enough).
- Use a soaker hose instead of a sprinkler.
- Let grass grow long, which protects roots from the heat.
- Get a push mower, and enjoy the exercise (www.reelmowerguide.com).

Advanced ways to reduce water use include graywater systems and rainwater harvesting. A graywater system reuses water from showers and washing machines to flush the toilet and water lawns and gardens. Rainwater harvesting means collecting the water running off your roof and using it for gardening, flushing your toilet, and laundry. In Australia, rainwater harvesting helped several communities defer hundreds of millions of dollars in infrastructure costs. Some Australian cities, including Adelaide, require all new homes to have plumbed rainwater tanks. In Germany, government subsidies and education programs helped make rainwater harvesting popular. Austin, Texas, sells rainbarrels below cost and offers a rebate of up to $500 to people who install a rainwater harvesting system.

### Repair

A tap that leaks one drop per second will waste close to 9,000 liters (2,000 gallons) in a year. A toilet that runs is even worse, wasting as much as 328,500 liters a year. Although plumbers are expensive, you'll save more money from lower utility bills than you'll pay to fix water leaks. If you're handy, tackle minor repairs by yourself. To detect leaks, read your water meter before and after a two-hour period when no water is used. If the meter reading isn't exactly the same, you have a leak. Check your toilet

## SOME GREEN ICING ON THE ENERGY-SAVINGS CAKE

Not only will reducing energy and water use save you money, many governments and utilities will pay you to make the changes. Federal, state, national, provincial, and local governments offer rebates and tax credits on everything from weather stripping and solar water heaters to low-flow toilets and taps. There are many different incentive programs, with payments ranging into the thousands of dollars. To find out which programs are available to you, check out the following resources.

AUSTRALIA
*Federal rebates:* www.greenhouse.gov.au/rebates/index.html
*Local information on rebates and incentives:* www.savewater.com.au

CANADA
*Environment Canada incentives and rebates:*
www.incentivesandrebates.ca/gc_fi_search.asp
*Natural Resources Canada grants and incentives:*
http://oee.nrcan.gc.ca/corporate/incentives.cfm?attr=4

U.K.
*Grants and offers:* www.energysavingtrust.org.uk
*Low carbon building grants:* www.lowcarbonbuilding.org.uk

U.S.
*The Database of State Incentives for Renewables and Efficiency:*
www.dsireusa.org
*Federal tax breaks related to home energy:* www.energy.gov/taxbreaks.htm
*Federal tax incentives for energy-efficient products and technologies:*
www.energytaxincentives.org

for leaks by adding food coloring to the tank. If the toilet is leaking, color will appear in the bowl within fifteen minutes. Flush as soon as the test is done, since food coloring may stain the bowl. Most replacement parts are inexpensive, readily available, and easily installed. For an excellent online primer on toilet repair, see www.toiletology.com.

## Replace

Homes in many parts of the industrialized world still have inefficient water fixtures and appliances. Replacing wasteful toilets, showerheads, faucets, clothes washers, and dishwashers with efficient versions can reduce water use by up to 75%. The U.S. Congress passed National Plumbing Standards in 1992, requiring all new homes to install efficient, low-flow toilets (6 liters or 1.6 gallons per flush), showerheads (11 liters or 2.5 gallons per minute), and faucets (11 liters or 2.5 gallons per minute). Unfortunately, there are still lots of water guzzlers in older homes. Canada lags behind the U.S. in mandating efficient fixtures.

Toilets are the top priority. Older toilets generally use 13 to 20 liters (3 to 4 gallons) per flush but can use as many as 30 liters. One in four toilets sold today in Canada is still a water-wasting 13-liter model, causing more than 8 billion liters to be needlessly flushed annually. High-efficiency toilets use as little as 4.5 liters per flush. Another efficient option is the dual-flush toilet, which lets you choose how much water to use (6 liters or 3 liters). Dual-flush toilets are common in Australia and Europe. Not all toilets perform equally. See www.cwwa.ca or www.cuwcc.org for a regularly updated report on toilet performance.

It's amazing how much money efficient water fixtures can save. If you switch from a standard toilet (19 liters) to a low-flow model (6 liters) you may save more than $100 per year, and reduce your water use by more than 75,000 liters. Switching to a high-efficiency toilet can save an additional 12,000 liters and $20. New ultra-low-flow showerheads can save $35 to $70 per year on water costs, depending on how often you shower and for how long. Australia offers a water efficiency labeling scheme to help citizens make the best choices when it comes to dish-washers, clothes washers, taps, and toilets. As water and energy prices rise, so will the amount of money you save by owning more efficient appliances. When it's time for a new clothes washer, look for an energy-efficient front-loading machine. Front-loading washing machines use less than half the water of top-loaders, cause less wear and tear on cloth-ing, and decrease drying time by wringing out more water during the spin cycle. Because they use relatively little water, front-loaders also reduce the energy needed for heating water by more than 50%.

## Inspiration

Many communities have saved hundreds of millions of dollars by pur-suing efficiency and conservation initiatives instead of expanding water storage, treatment, and distribution infrastructure. Faced with estimated costs of $125 million for a new water supply, Durham, Ontario, imple-mented a comprehensive ten-year efficiency program instead, at a cost of just $17 million. New York, Boston, Seattle, and Albuquerque reduced water use by 25% to 30% by implementing conservation programs. St. Petersburg, Florida, was the first major American city to close the loop completely by reusing all of its wastewater—discharging none to local rivers, lakes, or streams. Wastewater, after being treated, is used for irri-gating lawns, parks, and other municipal green spaces.

## RECAP

Improving energy and water efficiency are good investments, not sacri-fices. On the energy side, get a professional energy audit and follow the recommendations. Implement as many of our no- and low-cost changes as you can, starting with turning down the thermostats on your fur-nace and hot water heater. Always purchase the most energy-efficient appliances and electronics. Make the switch to green electricity, even if it means paying a modest premium. To save water, reduce, repair, and replace.

# ≡ GREEN BUILDING ≡

BUILDINGS designed to be green reduce ecological footprints and provide occupants with healthier, more comfortable spaces for living, working, and studying. Studies show that green buildings contribute to higher test results for students, higher sales in stores, increased productivity in offices and factories, and earlier discharges from hospitals. Green buildings enjoy higher market value, lower operating costs, less risk of obsolescence, and put less pressure on local infrastructure. Design and construction costs are either the same as or marginally higher (2% to 5%) than conventional buildings. Green buildings that meet LEED standards (Leadership in Energy and Environmental Design) gain financial benefits that are ten times the additional cost of green design and construction (increased market value, reduced energy and water use, and reduced insurance premiums).

### TIPS FOR BUILDING A GREEN HOME

· Avoid building a home bigger than you need.
· Choose a location that minimizes your need to drive.
· Renovate an existing building and reuse materials.
· Minimize construction waste.
· Select materials with low embodied energy (the amount of energy that went into making them).
· Use local materials.
· Use materials that can be easily separated for eventual reuse or recycling.
· Ensure that your home will be super energy efficient.
· Incorporate renewable energy.
· Use an integrated design process to set challenging targets for energy, water, and materials consumption, and to ensure a high-performance building.

Remarkable advances are being made in green building, with experts saying that "the best structures being built today would not have been possible ten years ago; the best structures we'll be able to build ten years from now may not even be imaginable today." Sustainable buildings sip water and energy instead of guzzling them, generate some or all of their own energy from clean, renewable sources, and are bright, comfortable places. Experts believe that by 2020 energy consumption in new housing can be reduced by up to 80% when compared with conventional construction. With existing homes, a reasonable target is to reduce energy use by one-half to two-thirds. Achieving these goals will be challenging but is possible—and would reduce energy use enough that rooftop solar panels (photovoltaic and thermal) could enable most homes to achieve zero energy performance.

# 3

# Food for Thought:
# Eating a Planet-friendly Diet

*Switching to a life of wild berry eating, interspersed*
*with the occasional grub or roasted squirrel, isn't necessary.*
DAVE REAY

❧   ❧   ❧

On the one hand, today's food system seems like an incredible success,
providing an unprecedented quantity of inexpensive food that's
available year-round no matter where you live. On the other hand,
from both health and environmental perspectives, something has gone
terribly wrong. Seduced by the siren songs of food corporations and their
multimillion-dollar marketing campaigns, confounded by the dazzling
variety of choices, and lured on by seemingly endless quantities of everything, many people living in industrialized nations eat diets that are
unhealthy for ourselves and the Earth. We drink rivers of soda pop and
eat mountains of junk food. In North America, we consume portions
that have doubled, tripled, and even quadrupled in size. We eat food
imported from the other side of the planet but throw away half the food
we purchase. We eat foods laced with pesticides, antibiotics, and hormones, and are blind to the ethical impacts of what we eat. Our industrial food system is responsible for a number of environmental effects:

- Raising livestock contributes more to climate change than the worldwide transportation sector.
- The use of chemical pesticides increased 600% in the U.S. during the latter half of the twentieth century.
- Worldwide, the use of chemical fertilizers tripled between 1945 and 1960, tripled again by 1970, and doubled again by 1980.
- Agriculture is a factor in the decline of more than half the species listed as endangered or threatened under the U.S. Endangered Species Act.
- The U.S. Environmental Protection Agency estimates that agriculture is responsible for 70% of the nation's water pollution.
- The Mississippi River creates a massive dead zone in the Gulf of Mexico by discharging vast volumes of manure, pesticides, and artificial fertilizers.
- Producing meat uses vast volumes of water. For example, beef requires up to 70,000 liters (15,400 gallons) per kilogram and chicken requires up to 6,000 liters (1,320 gallons) per kilogram.
- Cattle, pigs, and chickens produce approximately 5 tons of manure per North American per year.
- In the Amazon, millions of hectares of rainforest have been cut down for livestock grazing and feed crops since 1970.
- Globally, the volume of wild fish caught has increased almost 500% in the past fifty years, while populations of large fish—sharks, tuna, swordfish, and others—have crashed by 90%.
- More than ninety nations, including the U.S. and Canada, are guilty of overfishing, meaning that within their territorial waters they catch fish faster than fish populations can reproduce.
- Some types of fish farming pollute the marine environment with chemicals, pesticides, and antibiotics, and threaten the survival of wild stocks by spreading parasites and disease.

And not only the environment suffers because of our unsustainable food choices. Today's diets are making us sick, and in some cases, killing us. The U.S. Centers for Disease Control estimates that 76 million

Americans get sick, more than 325,000 are hospitalized, and 5,000 people die from foodborne illnesses each year. To put it another way, every day of the year 200,000 Americans are sickened by a foodborne disease, 900 are hospitalized, and 14 die. Fewer than 10% of Americans eat a healthy diet. The diet-related medical costs of six health conditions—coronary heart disease, cancer, stroke, diabetes, hypertension, and obesity—are roughly $100 billion per year.

## WHAT YOU CAN DO

The key determinants of the ecological footprint of food are agricultural or fishing practices, processing, transportation, packaging, and household activities (e.g., refrigeration, cooking). Current western diets cause environmental impacts that are four times greater than the sustainable level, meaning we need to significantly reduce the ecological footprint of the food we eat. By eating a local, organic, and predominantly plant-based diet you can reduce the ecological footprint of the food you eat by as much as 90%. And your health will get a big boost too. There are six simple changes that can dramatically reduce your diet's ecological footprint:

1. Eating less meat, eggs, and dairy products.
2. Choosing local food.
3. Buying organic products.
4. Favoring whole foods over processed foods.
5. Consuming fewer calories.
6. Avoiding bottled water.

### EAT LESS MEAT, EGGS, AND DAIRY PRODUCTS

*The greatness of a nation and its moral progress can be judged by the way its animals are treated.*—MAHATMA GANDHI

Meat, eggs, and dairy products are the most environmentally damaging foods that most people consume. Reducing the amount of meat, eggs, and dairy you eat doesn't mean that you have to become a vegetarian or a vegan, although these are environmentally friendly, financially smart, and healthy options. Vegetarians do not eat flesh, fowl, or fish. Vegans go one step further and do not eat eggs or dairy products. To get started on a less meaty diet, you can:

· Eat smaller portions of meat and dairy.
· Eat meat and dairy less frequently.
· Replace meat with products that look and taste like meat but are made of plant protein (e.g., veggie burgers).
· Experiment with vegetarian meals at home and in restaurants.
· Borrow a vegan or vegetarian cookbook from the library.
· Try meat-free Mondays.

Although some people worry that a vegetarian diet provides insufficient protein, these concerns are unfounded. Medical professionals now recognize that plant-based diets improve health and reduce risks of disease. Vegetarian sources of protein include:

· Nuts and seeds: hazelnuts, Brazil nuts, almonds, cashews, walnuts, sesame seeds, pumpkin seeds, hemp seeds, sunflower seeds.
· Legumes: beans (black beans, kidney beans, navy beans, lima beans, soy beans, chickpeas), peas (green and yellow peas, black-eyed peas), lentils, peanuts.
· Grains and cereals: rice, wheat, millet, quinoa, barley, buckwheat, corn, spelt, kamut, oats, rye, amaranth.
· Leafy green vegetables: spinach, kale, collard greens, seaweed, kelp.
· Soy products: tofu, tempeh, soy milk.
· Dairy products: eggs, cheese, milk, yogurt.

Some plant proteins are incomplete and need to be combined with other proteins. Examples of healthy complete protein combinations include corn and beans, nut butter and whole grain bread, and rice with lentils or split peas. As long as you eat a wide variety of healthy foods you'll get sufficient protein.

If you do continue to eat meat, eggs, and dairy products, healthier options for both people and the planet involve livestock that is raised

## TRY SOME MOUTH-WATERING, PLANET-FRIENDLY FOOD

### SESAME BAKED TOFU

1 block extra firm organic tofu

15 milliliters (1 tablespoon) organic tamari or soy sauce

30 milliliters (2 tablespoons) sesame oil

15 milliliters (1 tablespoon) grated ginger

Cracked pepper

Sesame seeds

Cut the tofu into 1-centimeter (1/2-inch) squares and mix with remaining ingredients. Spread on a cookie sheet and bake at 180°C (350°F) for 20 to 25 minutes. Serve with steamed vegetables and rice with peanut sauce.

### VEGETARIAN COOKBOOKS

M. Katzen, *The New Moosewood Cookbook* (Ten Speed Press, 2000)

A. Alsterburg and W. Urbanowicz, *Rebar Modern Food Cookbook* (Big Ideas Publishing, 2001)

D. Madison, *Vegetarian Cooking for Everyone* (Broadway, 1997)

M. Jaffrey, *World Vegetarian: More than 650 Meatless Recipes from Around the World* (Clarkson Potter, 2002)

P. Berley, *Fresh Food Fast: Delicious, Seasonal Vegetarian Meals in Under an Hour* (William Morrow, 2004)

### VEGAN COOKBOOKS

I.C. Moskowitz, *Vegan with a Vengeance: Over 150 Delicious, Cheap, Animal-Free Recipes That Rock* (Marlowe and Company, 2005)

M. Reinfeld and B. Rinaldi, *Vegan World Fusion Cuisine: Over 200 Award-winning Recipes* (Thousand Petals Publishing, 2005)

R. Robertson, *Vegan Planet: 400 Irresistible Recipes with Fantastic Flavors from Home and Around the World* (Harvard Common Press, 2003)

D. Klein, *The Mediterranean Vegan Kitchen* (HP Trade, 2001) responsibly—that is, by a local farmer, using organic, free-range, and grass-fed practices without hormones and antibiotics (see www.eatwell guide.org and www.eatwild.com). Your best source of information will be a local butcher or local farmers. Generally speaking, the production of beef causes the most environmental damage, followed by the production of pork and chicken. Raising a kilogram (2.2 pounds) of beef can generate the equivalent amount of carbon dioxide emitted by the average European car every 250 kilometers (150 miles). Of course, you can take the advice to eat less meat with a grain of salt if you live a subsistence lifestyle or reside in a place where climate or geography limits your culinary options (e.g., the Arctic or the Kalahari Desert).

If you choose to eat seafood, and some types of seafood offer substantial health benefits, ensure that you are selecting a sustainably harvested and uncontaminated species. Mercury contamination is a problem affecting large marine species (e.g., tuna, swordfish, and shark) and many kinds of sport fish caught in North American lakes. To help you make the right decisions, convenient and regularly updated lists of good seafood choices are compiled by environmental organizations throughout the world. See the Monterey Bay Aquarium's guide (www.seafood watch.org), Canada's Seafood Guide (www.seachoice.org), Australia's sustainable seafood guide (www.amcs.org.au), or the U.K.'s sustainable seafood directory (www.fishonline.org).

How big a difference will a predominantly plant-based diet make in terms of reducing the ecological footprint of the food you eat? Producing animal protein requires ten times as much energy and produces ten times as many greenhouse gas emissions as plant protein. Compared with plant protein, red meat is responsible for six to twenty times the land use, five to seventeen times the water pollution, and five to twenty-five times the water use. Similarly, catching fish using trawlers consumes fourteen times as much energy as growing vegetable protein. Therefore switching to a predominantly plant-based diet could reduce your ecological footprint from eating by up to 90%. To put these statistics in context, consider that the average American meat-based diet generates nearly

### BEST CHOICES
(there are no concerns; products are fished or farmed
in an environmentally responsible way):

Catfish (U.S. farmed), Clams (farmed),
Halibut (wild, Pacific), Pollock (wild, Alaska),
Rainbow trout (farmed), Tilapia (U.S. farmed)

### CONSUME INFREQUENTLY
(there are some environmental or health concerns):

Catfish (international farmed),
Clams (wild, Atlantic soft shell, Pacific geoduck), Crab (king, snow),
Lobster (American, Atlantic), Squid

### AVOID
(there are serious environmental or health concerns):

Chilean seabass/Patagonian toothfish, Cod (Atlantic), Monkfish,
Orange roughy, Rockfish, Salmon (farmed), Shark, Tuna (bluefin)

### THE WILD SALMON DILEMMA

Making a recommendation about eating wild salmon is difficult because
not all wild salmon populations are in the same shape and their status
often changes from year to year. For example, in 2007, Canadian fisheries
experts identified Nass River sockeye and seine-caught pink salmon as "better" choices, while chinook salmon and Fraser River sockeye were classified
as "poor" choices. Unfortunately, this information is not generally found on
labels, so the best advice for wild salmon lovers is to regularly check www.
seafoodwatch.org and www.seachoice.org and ask stores and restaurants
where their salmon comes from.

1.5 tons more carbon dioxide per year than a vegan diet, similar to the difference in annual emissions between driving a regular car and a hybrid. Changing your diet could make a bigger difference in reducing your ecological footprint than changing your vehicle.

Another compelling reason to cut back on meat consumption is your health. Eating less meat reduces your risk of chronic health problems: heart disease, stroke, obesity, hypertension, cancer, gallbladder disease, and diabetes. The health benefits of reducing your consumption of meat, eggs, and dairy products also include:

· Lowering your risk of infection from pathogens such as *E. coli* 0157:H7, *Salmonella, Listeria, Toxoplasma*, and *Campylobacter*, which cause the majority of foodborne illnesses.

· Reducing your risk of infectious diseases linked to industrialized meat production such as bird flu, swine flu, and bovine spongiform encephalopathy (BSE, better known as mad cow disease).

Another health problem associated with meat consumption stems from the intensive application of antibiotics to livestock. More than half of all antibiotics used in North America are fed to livestock, and 90% are administered to make animals grow faster, not to treat infections. The inappropriate use of antibiotics in livestock is contributing to the emergence of antibiotic-resistant bacteria that can be transmitted to humans. Antibiotic resistance causes an increase in deaths and long-term illnesses, heightens the risk of global epidemics, and adds to health care expenses.

Cutting back on meat consumption is also the right thing to do ethically. The amount of grain fed to livestock in the U.S. could feed about 840 million people on a plant-based diet. If everyone in the world ate meat as voraciously as Americans, the planet could only support a human population of 2.5 billion people. To sustain today's levels of seafood consumption, we would need 2.5 times the world's oceans. By eating less meat, eggs, and dairy and switching to food raised in a sustainable way, you also reduce the inhumane treatment of animals on factory farms and in slaughterhouses.

Global trends indicate we need to reduce meat consumption now. Meat consumption quintupled in the last fifty years and is expected to double again in the decades ahead. Scientists are worried that by 2030 the world will be unable to produce enough grain to feed the livestock required to meet soaring demand for meat. If present seafood eating trends continue, experts fear that all fish stocks being commercially exploited today will be driven to the point of collapse by 2048.

## Inspiration

About 4% of Canadians and Americans are vegetarians. Notable vegetarians, past and present, include Leonardo da Vinci, Pythagoras, Albert Einstein, Leo Tolstoy, Gandhi, Benjamin Franklin, Steve Jobs, and Dave Scott (six-time winner of Hawaii's Ironman Triathlon). Benjamin Franklin said a vegetarian diet brought a "greater clearness of head and quicker comprehension." George Bernard Shaw said "A mind of the caliber of mine cannot derive its nutriment from cows." A recent study in the British Medical Journal concluded that children with above average intelligence were more likely to become vegetarians as adults.

### EAT LOCAL

Eating local is an act of rebellion against a food system that's detached from any notion of ecological reality. Chives grown in England are harvested, flown to Kenya, wrapped around vegetables grown in that African nation, and then flown back to England to be sold in supermarkets. Seafood harvested on the west coast of North America is shipped to China for processing and then shipped back to the U.S. and Canada. Because of globalization, food is often swapped, meaning a country exports and imports the same item. Canada exports bottled water to the U.S., Europe, and Africa and imports bottled water from the same places. In California, strawberry imports from Mexico peak during the California strawberry season.

The term food miles describes the distance that food items travel from producers to consumers. A pioneering study found that food items purchased in Chicago supermarkets traveled an average of 2,400 kilometers (1,500 miles), thirty-three times the distance traveled by food items in local food programs. The supermarket food items used four to seventeen times more fuel and caused five to seventeen times more greenhouse gas emissions than the locally produced foods. Similarly, a food miles study comparing seven dinner items bought at a Toronto, Ontario, farmers' market and similar items bought at a supermarket found that the local foods traveled an average of 101 kilometers (63 miles) while the supermarket foods traveled an average of 5,364 kilometers (3,326 miles). The imported foods caused up to one thousand times more greenhouse gas emissions than the local foods. Transporting half a kilogram (a pound) of fresh New Zealand lamb to Toronto by plane produces over 8 kilograms (18 pounds) of carbon dioxide, compared with the 7 grams (0.25 ounces) of carbon dioxide produced while trucking lamb from a local farm.

Despite rising energy costs, food miles are skyrocketing. China is now the second leading source of Canadian food imports after the U.S., raising concerns about food safety. Food that travels by air from far-flung places carries the largest ecological footprint, because of the energy, greenhouse gas emissions, and other pollutants involved. Yet air transport of food is increasing rapidly.

Eating local food is a wonderful way to reduce your food miles, reconnect with the rhythms of nature, and reduce your diet's ecological footprint. Local food also requires little packaging because less travel and time are needed to get the food to your plate. The food is fresher, more nutritious, and tastes better. Additional advantages include:

· You can support local farmers who want to offer varieties of produce bred for taste and freshness instead of long shelf life.
· You can support the preservation of diverse heirloom and heritage varieties of produce and livestock.
· You can keep your money in the local economy.
· You can help another endangered species—the family farm.

Signs in the store and labels are basic sources of information about where food comes from. Look for the words "Grown in" or "Made in" followed by the name of your country, region, or local area. Don't be fooled when the label says "Imported by" followed by the name of a local company. This indicates the product may come from far afield. As well, labels on food can be misleading. In Canada, people assume that produce labeled "BC Hothouse" (a popular brand) is from British Columbia. In fact, BC Hothouse is the corporation's name, and some of their produce is grown in Mexico and the U.S. Regulations governing food labels in some jurisdictions can also create another problem by allowing products to be labeled "Made locally" when a majority of the value is added from one local source. For example, in Canada, apple juice made from Chinese apples and Canadian water can be labeled "Product of Canada." Loopholes afflict food labeling in the U.S. as well, with wild fish being identified according to the origin of the fishing boat rather than where the fish were caught. Thus a tuna caught off the coast of South America by an American fishing boat would have "U.S.A." on the label.

In general, it is easier to find local food at smaller grocery stores than supermarket chains, although companies like Whole Foods are exceptions to the rule. Grocery store managers are generally receptive to customer requests to carry more local products, so ask for specific items that you'd like to purchase. Other ways to eat local food include:

· Shopping at farmers' markets.
· Purchasing food through community supported agriculture (CSA) initiatives.
· Growing food on your own property or at a community garden.

Farmers' markets are experiencing a period of explosive growth, fueled by people's dissatisfaction with industrial food. In the U.S., the number of farmers' markets doubled between 1994 and 2004. At farmers' markets you'll find a diverse assortment of fabulous fresh and seasonal foods, including fruit, vegetables, artisanal cheeses, and sustainably produced meats. To find the nearest farmers' market in your area, use the Internet and local newspaper listings. In the U.S., you can go to www.localharvest.org. In Canada, farmers markets are listed province by province (e.g., in British Columbia see www.bcfarmersmarket.org and in Ontario see www.farmersmarketsontario.com). In Australia, you can go to www.farmersmarkets.org.au. In the U.K., you can go to www.farmers markets.net.

Community supported agriculture programs enable people to become partners with farmers. You pay for weekly home delivery of a box filled with fresh, seasonal produce, providing a steady income to farmers and a cornucopia of delicious foods for you and your family. It's like being a shareholder, but instead of money your dividends are taste, freshness, nutrition, getting to know a local farmer, and peace of mind. Japanese women started the CSA movement in the 1970s because of concerns about chemical-laced foods and the decline of family farms. The first American CSA program debuted in 1985 and there are now more than one thousand in North America. To find CSA programs in the U.S. and Canada, go to www.localharvest.org or www.biodynamics.com. In Quebec, see www.equiterre.qc.ca. In the U.K., see www.cuco.org.uk. In Australia, see www.organicfooddirectory.com.au/comm_food.php.

The ultimate act of eating local, as well as the most satisfying, is to grow your own food. Fruit trees and bushes require minimal maintenance and can produce an annual bounty of sweet, fresh fruit. Even a small garden in a backyard or an apartment balcony can produce delicious herbs, strawberries, or cherry tomatoes. Many fruits and vegetables, including corn and apples, now come in dwarf varieties (referring to the plant, not the fruit). One useful approach if you have limited space is container gardening, meaning growing food and flowers in pots, bowls, and almost any container that can hold dirt and water. If you have a yard, consider digging up part or all of the lawn and planting things you can eat. Growing your own food will recast your relationship with soil, increase your appreciation for farmers, enhance awareness of the seasons, and even make you wish for rain.

If you live in a city and your home has no room for a garden, don't give up. Another fast-growing local food movement involves community gardens, where a group of citizens get together to grow food on shared plots of land. In St. Petersburg, Russia, more than half of the city's 5 million residents grow food. In London, England, there are more than thirty thousand community or allotment gardeners. Check out the American Community Garden Association's website to find the closest community garden or get great advice on how to start one at www.communitygarden.org. In Canada, see www.canadiangardening.com. In Australia, see www.communitygarden.org.au. In the U.K., see www.allotment.org.uk.

There are exceptions to the rule that local food has a smaller environmental impact. For example, tomatoes and other foods raised in

## START AN ORGANIC VEGETABLE GARDEN

1. Choose a site with lots of sun and decide if you need a fence (for deer, geese, etc.).
2. Start small, as you can always expand later. A good size for a garden is 3 meters by 4.5 meters (10 feet by 15 feet).
3. Select plants that are easy to grow and delightful to eat fresh (e.g., lettuce, peas, tomatoes, carrots, beans, chard, zucchini).
4. Ask lots of questions of neighbors with green thumbs, and at the local nursery, garden store, and farmers' market (e.g., what thrives locally, when to plant, what to add to the soil).
5. Dig up the soil (you can test your soil if you have concerns about its quality, or to learn the ideal soil amendments for your garden).
6. Add a combination of topsoil, compost, and organic fertilizer.
7. Plant organic seeds and seedlings (following instructions on labels).
8. Thin out plants, weed as needed, and water regularly (adding mulch reduces weed growth and water use).
9. Watch for pests, and use organic methods of pest control.
10. Harvest and enjoy.

heated greenhouses in northern nations may be local but can have a large ecological footprint. As well, sometimes the "buy local" rule of thumb needs to give way to social considerations. Buying food from a developing nation may provide essential income for poor farmers and their communities. When you buy imported food, check for fair-trade certification. Fair-trade means that the people who grow, harvest, and handle your food are properly compensated and work in reasonably safe conditions. TransFair, the leading fair-trade certifier in Canada and the U.S., also includes environmental standards in its certification process. Fair-trade products that are widely available include coffee, chocolate, and bananas. Ambitious coffee drinkers can go for triple certified java— fair-trade, organic, and shade-grown (plantations protect bird habitat).

### Inspiration

How far can you take the local food idea? Alisa Smith and J.B. MacKinnon, two writers from Vancouver, B.C., lived for a full year on a "100-mile diet," eating (almost) nothing grown, raised, or processed beyond that self-imposed geographic limit. Although they encountered some vexing challenges along the way (e.g., no wheat, no sugar, no salt), they ate an imaginative and healthy diet. In the process they befriended local farmers and fishermen, and became intimately connected to the geography, climate, and environmental challenges of the Pacific Northwest.

American novelist Barbara Kingsolver, her husband, and two daughters lived for a year on a farm in Virginia, growing and raising most of their own food and occasionally buying local products. They canned, pickled, preserved, and froze food to get themselves through the winter. The average cost of a meal, excluding their labor, was well under $1.

Gary Paul Nabhan wrote a book about eating a diet limited to what could be grown, fished, or gathered within 400 kilometers (250 miles) of his Tucson, Arizona, home. Nabhan occasionally ate road-kill, which may be going a little bit farther than the average person wants to go in pursuit of a pro-environment diet.

Organic agriculture combines traditional farming methods with modern technology, while avoiding synthetic pesticides and fertilizers, genetically modified organisms, sewage sludge, and irradiation. Raising livestock organically eliminates the need to use growth hormones, antibiotics, and feed made with animal by-products. Organic agriculture emphasizes protecting and improving soil quality, rotating crops, controlling pests naturally, and raising a diversity of animals and plants. Food in Australia, Canada, the U.K., the U.S., and other western nations can only use the word organic on the label if it is certified by an accredited organization.

The main reason many people eat organic foods is to avoid pesticides. Pesticides are so heavily used today that detectable pesticide residues are found in the bodies of virtually every person living in North America, including newborn infants. Fifty years ago, 11% of American corn was treated with pesticides. Today, more than 95% is treated. Pesticide exposures are linked to increased risk of cancer; neurological impairment (e.g., Parkinson's disease, Alzheimer's disease); developmental effects (e.g., autism); reproductive effects (e.g., sperm abnormalities, birth defects); organ damage; and interference with the human hormone system. Pesticides can also have a devastating impact on wildlife and ecosystems. The U.S. Fish and Wildlife Service estimates that 67 million birds are killed in the U.S. annually by pesticides. Even Arctic ecosystems and national parks in the Rocky Mountains are contaminated by pesticide residues, which evaporate off farmers' fields a continent away, travel along jet streams, precipitate, and fall to Earth when they encounter a cold front.

Eating organic food clearly reduces the risks associated with pesticide exposure. A study published in 2006 demonstrated that when a group of children in Seattle, Washington, had their diet switched from conventional food (grown with pesticides) to organic food, pesticide residues in their urine quickly dropped to nondetectable levels. The authors of the study concluded that switching to an organic diet provides children with "immediate and dramatic" protection against the adverse health effects of exposure to pesticides. There is also some evidence that organic food is more nutritious than conventional food, offering better protein quality, and higher levels of antioxidants, vitamin C, and minerals (e.g., calcium, iron, zinc, and magnesium). There are other important health and environmental benefits of eating organic. Organic agriculture is better for biodiversity and leads to less water and air pollution. In addition, organic methods of production can:

· Save energy.
· Lower greenhouse gas emissions.
· Build healthier, more fertile soil.
· Be safer for farmers and farm workers.
· Avoid possible risks from genetically engineered foods.
· Avoid possible risks of applying sewage sludge to crops.
· Avoid use of intensive feedlots or factory farms for raising animals.

Most supermarkets and many smaller grocery stores carry organic products, and the trend is increasing. Sales of organic food are growing by more than 20% annually and are now about $20 billion in North America and more than $4 billion in the U.K. If you're looking for a particular organic product, ask your local store manager to stock it. The odds are that if you're looking for it, so are many other people. The American Organic Consumers Association offers a buyers' guide at www. organicconsumers.org/btc/BuyingGuide.cfm. In Australia, you can find a directory at www.organicfooddirectory.com.au. The Canadian Organic Growers offer a directory at www.cog.ca/buyorganic.htm. In the U.K., the Soil Association offers a directory at www.whyorganic.org.

When deciding which foods in your diet should be organic priorities, consider the following: meat, dairy, peaches, apples, sweet bell peppers, celery, nectarines, strawberries, cherries, lettuce, grapes, pears, spinach, and potatoes. Baby food of any kind should also be a priority.

The lowest pesticide concerns are associated with onions, avocados, frozen corn, mangos, pineapples, frozen peas, asparagus, kiwis, bananas, cabbage, broccoli, and eggplant. It's a good idea to always wash fresh produce, even if it is organic.

The biggest knock against organic food is the higher cost, and organic food is usually more expensive in the ordinary sense. But conventional food, while seemingly cheap, has many hidden costs, including environmental damage and health care expenses. Forty years ago, Americans spent 18% of their income on food and only 5% to 6% of their income on health care. Now Americans spend 9% of their income on food (the lowest proportion in the world) and 16% to 18% of their income on health care. Canadians now spend 11% of their income on food, down from 19% in the 1960s. Trends in Australia and the U.K. are similar.

By spending more money on good food we can increase our quality of life, protect the environment, and reduce health care expenses. In short, organic food is generally well worth the higher price.

However, organic choices may not always be preferable. The environmental impacts of long-distance air transport, deep-freezing, and greenhouse production may exceed the impacts of locally produced nonorganic food. A British study of 26 organic food items estimated that they traveled a total of more than 240,000 kilometers (148,800 miles) to get to the supermarket. Try to get in the habit of checking to see where your food comes from. Local and organic is the best option. The farther the organic food travels, the smaller its overall environmental benefit, and the more likely that local is a greener choice.

### Inspiration

The Edible Schoolyard program in Berkeley, California, founded by chef Alice Waters, involves growing organic vegetables on school grounds. Kids cultivate seeds, learn about the environment and nutrition, celebrate the harvest, and take pride in feeding themselves. They learn where food comes from and develop a connection to the land. The original Edible Schoolyard program has inspired many others.

In Italy, recent laws require local authorities to include locally and organically produced foods on school menus. These laws reinforce the healthy Mediterranean diet (less meat, more seasonal fruit and vegetables, fewer processed foods). Jamie Oliver, aka the Naked Chef, has revolutionized school food programs in England by demonstrating that healthy and sustainable alternatives are affordable and popular with children.

## EAT WHOLE FOODS

To further reduce your ecological footprint and improve your health, replace junk food, fast food, and other highly processed food with whole foods. Whole foods are fruits, vegetables, grains, nuts, seeds, beans, and legumes that have not been extensively refined or processed. An apple is a whole food, while applesauce, apple juice, and apple pie are not. Hot oatmeal is a whole food while Frosted Flakes are not. Whole foods, like local foods, require less packaging and less processing, saving on energy, greenhouse gas emissions, chemical use, and waste.

Nutritionists offer a simple principle—the more processed a food, the lower its nutritional value is likely to be. Avoid products with long lists of ingredients that you don't recognize and can't pronounce. If you need a degree in biochemistry to decipher ingredients, odds are the food is bad for you and the environment. You can limit your exposure to processed foods by minimizing time in the center aisles of the grocery store where processed foods predominate, choosing healthy snack foods, and being selective about when and where you eat meals away from home. When switching to whole foods, consider the following suggestions:

- Substitute raw nuts and seeds (e.g., almonds, pumpkin seeds) for potato chips and corn chips.
- Choose fresh fruit instead of juice, and when you do drink juice, remember that more pulp means more nutritional value is retained.
- Become a smoothie connoisseur, using a blender to combine fruit, ice, plain yogurt, and 100% fruit juice or plain soy milk.
- Snack on raw vegetables, such as carrots, cherry tomatoes, and sugar peas.

- Eat hot oatmeal for breakfast and jazz it up with dried fruits, nuts, and ground flax seeds or choose cold cereals that are high-fiber, whole-grain, and low in sugar.
- Choose whole potatoes or side salads instead of French fries and go easy on toppings and salad dressing.
- Eat 100% whole wheat bread instead of white bread.
- Buy plain yogurt and add your own fruit, as many flavored yogurt products are more like desserts than health foods.

Your health will benefit from eating more whole foods and less processed food. Diets rich in fresh fruits and vegetables reduce the risk of cancer. Yet one-third of the vegetable servings consumed by Americans consist of French fries, potato chips, and iceberg lettuce. To meet U.S. dietary guidelines, the average American would have to increase fruit consumption by 131%, dark green leafy and deep yellow vegetables by 333%, and legumes (e.g., dried beans, peas, and lentils) by 200%, while reducing intake of potatoes and other starchy vegetables by 38%, fats and oils by 36%, and added sugars by 63%. Diets based largely on fruit, vegetables, nuts, and whole grains also provide significant protection from cardiovascular disease. The majority of North Americans consume levels of salt—mostly from processed foods and snack foods—far in excess of what doctors recommend. Reducing salt intake can lower blood pressure and reduce the risk of cardiovascular disease by 25%.

Children have even more to gain from eating whole foods. Only 1% of American children eat diets meeting federal recommendations. More than 70% of young Canadian children and 80% of Australian teenagers fail to eat the recommended amount of fruits and vegetables. In the U.K., 92% of children eat too much saturated fat and 83% eat excessive amounts of sugar, while eating less than half of the recommended amount of fruit and vegetables. Changing these dismal dietary patterns is critical to reversing the dramatic rise in childhood obesity and diabetes.

*Inspiration*

The slow food movement started in Italy as a response to the industrialization of our food system. Slow food proponents argue that the food we eat should taste good and be produced in a way that does not harm the environment, animal welfare, or human health, and that its producers should receive fair compensation for their work. Slow food organizations are active throughout the world.

## CONSUME FEWER CALORIES

Another step to reduce your environmental impact from food is to consume fewer calories. You can do this by substituting higher quality foods (fruits, vegetables, whole grains, and nuts) for the harmful calories in junk food, fast food, and other heavily processed, energy-dense foods. Americans drink more than 200 liters (about 50 gallons) of soda pop annually, and consume an average of more than 27 kilograms (60 pounds) of high-fructose corn syrup per person annually. Reach for a glass of water instead of a bottle of pop, and save about 250 calories (a 591-milliliter bottle of Coke contains the equivalent of fifteen spoonfuls of sugar). Eat one helping instead of two and cut the calories in half. The benefits include better health, money saved (an organic apple generally costs less than a chocolate bar or bag of chips), and a smaller ecological footprint.

In many parts of the world, eating fewer calories goes against the grain. In western nations, people are eating more and more. In the U.K. between 1995 and 2006, caloric intake increased by 17%. The average American consumed 700 more calories daily in 2000 than in 1973. The average Canadian ate 18% more calories in 2002 than in 1991, largely because of rising fat consumption. Throughout the world the growth of caloric intake is partly the result of increased dependence on fast food and junk food, bigger portions (Table 6), and the rise of snacking.

The environmental benefits of consuming fewer calories stem from the fact that your ecological footprint literally becomes lighter, as the following examples demonstrate:

- Less land is required to grow crops and raise livestock.
- Less energy, chemicals, and materials are used in food processing, packaging, and transport.
- Less material is used to make clothing.
- Less waste is created.

The weight gained by Americans during the 1990s (an average of 4.5 kilograms or 10 pounds per adult) caused airlines to burn an extra 1,589 million liters (350 million gallons) of jet fuel annually, beginning in 2000. The increasing body weight of Americans is forcing airlines to impose more restrictive weight limits on luggage and forcing health care

## ADVICE FOR READING FOOD LABELS

- Avoid products with long lists of ingredients.
- Be wary of misleading information related to serving sizes. For example, nutritional information on a 591-milliliter (20-ounce) pop bottle is based on a 227-milliliter (8-ounce) serving, but most people drink the whole bottle.
- Limit your intake of added sugar and salt. Sugar comes in many guises on food labels, including sucrose, fructose, dextrose, corn syrup, HFCS (high-fructose corn syrup), fruit juice concentrates, honey, and molasses.
- Minimize consumption of artificial flavors, colors, additives, and sweeteners (e.g., aspartame, sucralose, and acesulfame-K).
- Choose products listing substantial levels of fiber, vitamins, omega fatty acids, and minerals on nutrition labels. Avoid products listing substantial levels of saturated fats, cholesterol, sodium, and sugars.
- Watch for bogus health claims like "cholesterol-free" (no plant-based foods contain cholesterol) or "0 grams of trans fats" on unhealthy foods such as potato chips.
- Avoid hydrogenated vegetable oils because of their trans fat, and try not to eat foods made with palm oil, as most of it comes from plantations that have destroyed tropical rainforest.

providers to buy bigger and more expensive equipment including ambulances and stretchers.

The health benefits of consuming fewer calories are substantial. If you are obese, losing weight will reduce your risk of heart attack and stroke, diabetes, hypertension, gallbladder disease, osteoarthritis of the knee, and endometrial cancer. Rates of obesity are skyrocketing throughout the industrialized world. In Australia and the U.K., two of every three men and one of every two women are overweight or obese. In the U.S., three of every five Americans are overweight or obese. The proportion of overweight children in the U.S. has tripled over the past twenty-five years, and more than 5 million Americans are now "super obese," meaning they qualify for the radical surgery called gastroplasty or stomach stapling, which reduces the size of the stomach to limit food intake.

TABLE 6. *Increased portion sizes in the U.S.*

| FOOD ITEM | CALORIES 20 YEARS AGO | CALORIES TODAY |
| --- | --- | --- |
| Bagel | 140 | 350 |
| Cheeseburger | 333 | 590 |
| Spaghetti and meatballs | 500 | 1,025 |
| Soda pop | 85 | 250 |
| French fries | 210 | 610 |
| Turkey sandwich | 320 | 820 |
| Muffin | 210 | 500 |
| Pepperoni pizza slice | 250 | 425 |
| Chicken Caesar salad | 390 | 790 |
| Popcorn | 270 | 630 |
| Cheesecake slice | 260 | 640 |
| Chocolate chip cookie | 55 | 275 |

In recent years there has been a tidal wave of bottled water sales. North Americans drink bottled water that has traveled halfway around the world, from the French Alps, from Fiji, and even from drought-ridden Ethiopia. Annually Americans drink more bottled water, almost 110 liters (30 gallons) per person, than any other beverage except soda pop. According to Statistics Canada, almost one-third of Canadian households drank primarily bottled water in 2006. In the U.K., each person drinks about 37 liters per year. But the Italians lead the world, drinking more than 200 liters per person per year.

Don't buy bottled water. You'll save money and protect the environment. Check out your tap water quality. Most public drinking water systems in industrialized nations produce annual reports on their water quality and are accountable to their customers. If you rely on a private water system, such as your own well, have your water quality tested regularly. If either published reports or test results indicate that you have water quality problems, installing a high-quality filter for your home is generally a better option than buying bottled water. Home filtration is less expensive, more effective, more convenient, and much more environmentally friendly. Learn more about water filters (http://thegreen guide.com/reports/product.mhtml?id=23&sec=2). To carry drinking water during your daily activities, use a stainless steel thermos, mug, or water bottle.

Bottled water does have its place—in emergencies, in humanitarian crises, and in places where tap water is untreated or there are legitimate reasons to be concerned about drinking water quality. However, bottled water is expensive, creates a large ecological footprint, and offers little in the way of health benefits when compared with tap water. Bottled water costs about one thousand times more than ordinary municipally treated tap water. Although water is a publicly owned resource, many governments give it away free to the corporations that dominate the bottled water industry. Ontario recently responded to public pressure to stop giving away water, but charges corporations only $3.71 per million liters.

Bottled water leads to more greenhouse gas emissions than tap water. Most plastic water bottles are made of polyethylene terephthalate, a petroleum-based plastic that is energy- and water-intensive to make and produces harmful by-products in the manufacturing process. According to the Pacific Institute, making water bottles uses 17 million barrels of oil and produces 2.5 million tons of carbon dioxide annually in the U.S. Although plastic water bottles are recyclable, in North America most end up in dumps.

From a health perspective, neither tap water nor bottled water is perfectly safe. According to Peter Gleick, one of the world's leading water experts, it is "impossible to say that bottled water offers any guaranteed improvement over tap water." Although recalls of bottled water for health reasons are rare, the U.S. Natural Resources Defense Council did find contaminants in 20% of the bottled water samples they tested. Among the contaminants were styrene, toluene, xylene, arsenic, and bacteria. A Canadian study found samples of bottled water that exceeded national drinking water guidelines for lead, chloride, and total dissolved solids. And potentially harmful chemicals in the plastic water bottles themselves, including antimony and bisphenol A (BPA), can leach into the water over time. Antimony and its compounds can cause adverse health effects similar to arsenic. BPA is a known endocrine disruptor and may contribute to prostate cancer, miscarriage, and ovarian disease. Unlike in Europe, where the rules governing bottled water are quite strict, regulations in both the U.S. and Canada are weaker for bottled water than tap water, meaning there is less protection for the health of citizens.

Another problem is that growing demand for bottled water undermines confidence in public drinking water systems. In most jurisdictions in the industrialized world, tap water quality is adequate and is closely monitored by health authorities. If the tens of billions of dollars spent on bottled water annually were spent on improving drinking water infrastructure, then people and the environment would be far better off. And awareness of this is growing. Popular restaurants everywhere are taking bottled water off the menu. San Francisco no longer allows taxpayers' money to be spent on bottled water, Chicago has approved a tax of ten cents on every bottle, and organizations such as the United Church of Canada are urging their members not to buy bottled water.

## RECAP

More and more people recognize that a sustainable diet is good for personal and planetary health. It's encouraging to see rapidly increasing sales of organic food, heightened interest in farmers' markets and community supported agriculture, and a growing number of vegetarians (particularly young people). At the same time, it's clear that the industrial food system is wreaking havoc on the planet and urgently needs an overhaul. You can contribute to the shift that's underway. Because we eat three or more times daily, we have many opportunities to change our diets. Start gradually. You could begin by following one of our recommendations each week, or by shifting the way you consume a specific meal, such as lunch or breakfast. Eating home-cooked meals with family and friends is a great idea. We're not preaching food fundamentalism. You can still eat sinfully sugary snacks, go to a fast food outlet for a transfusion of fat, buy food from the far side of the planet, or give in to a craving for meat. In a sustainable future, however, these choices will be the exception rather than the rule.

The three most effective actions for reducing the ecological footprint of your diet are eating less meat, eggs, and dairy products, eating local, and choosing organic. Through these three simple actions, you can reduce greenhouse gas emissions, exposure to toxic substances, air and water pollution, and waste. By making these and three additional changes—eating more whole foods, consuming fewer calories, and avoiding bottled water—you can reduce your diet's ecological footprint by up to 90%. You can also achieve substantial health benefits, save money, support family farms and the local economy, and reduce the inhumane treatment of animals.

Recent experience with cigarette smoking demonstrates that major lifestyle changes can be achieved in a short time. The proportion of adult smokers in the U.S. dropped by 50% between 1965 and 2001 because of anti-smoking campaigns, mandatory warning labels, and public education about the adverse health effects of smoking. As a result, lung cancer rates are falling. Changes in today's diet are essential for improving public health and reducing environmental impacts. Eating is an agricultural act, a biological act, a social act, an economic act, and a political act. With every meal you can vote for the food system you would like to see.

# 4

## Traveling Light

*If I had asked people what they wanted,*
*they would have said faster horses.*
HENRY FORD

❧   ❧   ❧

Transportation caused environmental problems long before the automobile age. Only a century ago, horses were a major source of urban pollution. In New York, an estimated 1.1 million kilograms (2.5 million pounds) of manure and 272,400 liters (60,000 gallons) of urine hit the streets daily in 1900. Citizens complained about dust from pulverized horse dung blowing into their faces and homes. Manure piles were fertile ground for flies spreading infectious diseases. The combination of manure and rain created quagmires in the streets. Dead horses were also a problem, with New York removing fifteen thousand horse carcasses from its streets annually in the 1880s.

Despite these difficulties, the emergence of motor vehicles initially inspired fear and loathing. Great Britain passed a law requiring all motor vehicles to be preceded by a man on foot waving a red flag or lantern and blowing a horn. The law set speed limits of 6 kilometers (3 miles) an hour in the country and 3 kilometers (2 miles) an hour in cities. In 1875, the U.S. Congress warned that "horseless carriages propelled by gasoline engines might attain speeds of 14 or even 20 miles per hour... hurtling through our streets and poisoning our atmosphere." In 1900, there was only one car for every ten thousand Americans, and the first flight was still a twinkle in the Wright brothers' eyes. Cars didn't outnumber horses in New York, London, or Paris until 1912.

Today, the largest transportation footprints in the world belong to Americans and Canadians. Cars outnumber drivers in the U.S., and there are more American households with four vehicles than with none. Canadians and Americans produce about 6 tons of carbon dioxide per person in transport emissions, three times the European average. The average household has fewer people but owns more vehicles (especially gas-guzzling SUVs and trucks) and takes more than one hundred additional vehicle trips per year compared with 1990. Between 80% and 90% of trips are taken by a driver alone or a driver with one passenger. Public transit trips have fallen dramatically in Canada since the late 1950s, from approximately two hundred and fifty trips per person per year to approximately fifty. Similarly, in Australia, trips by rail accounted for 40% of urban travel in 1945. Cars now predominate and only 4% of trips are by rail.

Today's cars are inefficient, depend on nonrenewable fossil fuels, and are a major cause of deadly air pollution and climate change. Less than 1% of the energy in gasoline moves the driver; the rest either moves the car or is wasted. We build cities for cars, not people, resulting in congestion, noise, ugly urban landscapes, and deaths and injuries from accidents. More Americans have died in traffic accidents than in all the wars the United States has fought during its history.

Our transportation habits cause a host of problems, including:
· Water pollution, smog, and heavy metal contamination.
· Almost one-third of greenhouse gas emissions in both Canada and the U.S.
· Tens of thousands of deaths annually from heart and lung diseases.
· The dripping, leaking, and spilling of more oil every year than the *Exxon Valdez* oil spill in Alaska.
· The death of tens of millions of animals annually in collisions, from moose to turtles, and the injury of many millions more.

Urban sprawl, which is closely linked to car-centered transport systems, causes a host of problems as well, including:

- High infrastructure costs (road construction and maintenance, water and sewer pipelines, electricity and telecommunication services).
- Congestion.
- Longer commuting distances and times.
- Social isolation.
- Loss of valuable agricultural land, wildlife habitat, and green space.

Future generations may well look back at the internal combustion engine and our addiction to cars with the same mix of disbelief and scorn we exhibit for the thought of a transport system dominated by horses.

## WHAT YOU CAN DO

The environmental destruction wrought by the contemporary transport system comes from the accumulation of individual decisions made by millions of people. Driving and flying contribute the most to the average ecological footprint of people throughout the industrialized world. By making different transport choices, you can reduce pollution, accidents, and congestion, improve your health and happiness, save money, and help tip the balance towards a more sustainable world.

There are five effective ways you can reduce your impacts from both ground and air travel by as much as 90%:

1. Consciously taking travel into consideration when deciding where to live.
2. Driving and flying less by relying on alternatives such as cycling, walking, rollerblading, better planning, public transit, car sharing, carpooling, home delivery of groceries, videoconferencing, and telecommuting.
3. Buying the most fuel-efficient vehicle possible.
4. Improving your driving habits.
5. Switching to cleaner fuels.

The massive environmental, economic, and social costs of transport reinforce the importance of making smart, ecologically informed decisions about where you live. The ideal location is close to work, schools, friends, recreation, and stores or close to effective public transit. According to mobility experts, if you have to travel more than twenty minutes to work, either your residence or your job is in the wrong place. While housing closer to work, school, and so on may appear expensive, it is important to take the costs of transport and commuting (in terms of time, money, and quality of life) into consideration when deciding where to live.

### DRIVE AND FLY FEWER KILOMETERS

North Americans rack up more than 8 trillion "passenger kilometers" per year on the road and in the air. It's hard to imagine the immensity of something measured in trillions. Eight trillion kilometers represents 200 million trips around the Earth at the equator or 21 million trips to the moon. Put another way, the average North American driver circumnavigates the planet every year and a half. The most fundamental change that individuals can make is to drive and fly less frequently. This isn't an ecological version of house arrest because there are many effective and life-enhancing ways to reduce your road and air kilometers.

### *Inspiration*

A walking schoolbus is a group of children walking to school together under adult supervision. Parents, teachers, and police map where children live and identify the safest route to school. Adults in the community then volunteer as walking bus "drivers" who walk a fixed route, "picking up" kids and delivering them safely to school. The benefits include increased physical activity (and reduced risk of childhood obesity), less traffic congestion, safer streets, and improved air quality. Walking schoolbus programs are sprouting up all over Australia (www.travel smart.gov.au/schools/index.html), the U.K. (www.foe.co.uk/campaigns/

transport/resource/parents.html), the U.S. (www.saferoutesinfo.org), and Canada. See www.walkingschoolbus.org for more general information.

### Cycling, Walking, and Other Self-propelled Approaches

The most pro-environmental ways to travel are by walking, cycling, roller-blading, paddling, or otherwise using your own energy. Self-propelled transport burns no fossil fuels, produces no harmful emissions, and incurs minimal costs. Bicycles are the most efficient form of transportation (see Table 7). Cycling and walking in Australia, Canada, Europe, and the U.S. already save billions of liters of gasoline, millions of tons of carbon dioxide emissions, and millions of tons of other air pollutants every year. In many European cities, such as Paris, Amsterdam, Copenhagen, and Stockholm, cycling and walking have a long tradition and are increasingly popular. Although your grocery bills may go up, your savings on transport costs will be much larger. You'll reap the added benefit of getting exercise. Many people dismiss active forms of transport as impractical, and in some circumstances (during winter cold spells, for long commutes) they're right. However studies show that half of vehicle trips taken in the U.S. are for very short distances—5 kilometers (3 miles) or less. Trips of this distance can easily be done by biking or walking, and are a good place to start decreasing your dependence on cars.

The popularity of cycling has surged in recent years, with the number of trips taken by bicycle in the U.S. doubling over the past decade. More bicycles are now sold in Canada and the U.S. each year than motor vehicles. Investment in bike paths and designated cycling routes is growing. Walking schoolbus programs offer a safe, healthy, and fun way for children to be supervised on a walk to school. In the U.S., the number of walking and bicycling trips doubled between 1990 and 2001 (to more than 35 billion). Every person who switches some travel to cycling and walking adds to the momentum. In Australia, Canada, the U.K., and the U.S., only 1% of all trips are by bicycle, so there is lots of room for improvement. In Germany and Sweden, 10% of all trips are by bicycle, a figure that rises to 18% in Denmark, and to 27% in the Netherlands.

Consider the following tips for walkers and cyclists:

- Go for a couple of test trips to assess, realistically, what's within a reasonable range of your home. You may be surprised how many places are within walking or cycling distance.
- Check out possible routes on a map. Sometimes an indirect route allows you to avoid heavy traffic or enjoy a nice path or great scenery.
- Invest in good gear. Comfortable shoes are vital for walkers, while a lightweight and properly fitted bicycle is a great investment. Windproof, waterproof, and breathable clothing will increase your comfort level.
- Do a trial run on a day off to get a sense of how long trips will take without the pressure of having to be on time.
- Start slow so that your body has time to adapt. Try going car-free one day a week. You might be able to walk or ride one way and then take public transit on the return trip.
- Keep a change of clothing and shoes at work or school.
- Be safe. Walk or ride defensively. Always wear a helmet when cycling. Use essential safety equipment such as lights and reflectors.
- Carry a water bottle and pack a snack for longer distances.
- Expand the range of your potential activities by investing in a comfortable knapsack or wheeled cart for walking and panniers or a trailer for cycling.

Perhaps the most compelling argument in favor of walking and cycling is that these modes of travel will make you happier. People who cycle and walk to work enjoy commuting whereas most drivers are stressed and dissatisfied. Many cyclists rate their journey to and from work as one of the best parts of their day.

### Inspiration

Copenhagen, the capital of Denmark, consistently ranks among the top cities in the world for its high quality of life. One in three persons commutes to work by bicycle, and there are more than 300 kilometers

(200 miles) of bicycle paths. The City Bikes program offers more than one thousand distinctive-looking bikes for free use in downtown. Copenhagen plans to double its spending on cycling infrastructure over the next three years.

In Amsterdam, 40% of commuters get to work by bike, and the municipal government is building a new parking garage for ten thousand bikes at the main train station. Sweden aims to raise bicycle traffic from 12% to 16% of all travel by 2010, while Norway hopes to double bicycle trips from 4% to 8% of all trips by 2015.

TABLE 7. *Energy used by various modes of transport*

| MODE OF TRANSPORT | CALORIES BURNED PER KILOMETER | CALORIES BURNED PER MILE |
|---|---|---|
| Cycling | 22 | 35 |
| Walking | 62 | 100 |
| Driving in an automobile | 1,155 | 1,860 |

### Better Planning

Americans make a mind-boggling 1.1 billion vehicle trips per day—an average of four trips per person. Forty-five percent of trips are taken for shopping and errands, 27% are for social or recreational activities, and 15% involve commuting. Better planning could eliminate many time-wasting trips. Key questions to ask yourself are:

· Do I really need to make this trip by car?
· What are my alternatives?
· What changes would enable me to avoid making this trip by car?

Modest changes to travel patterns can cut time spent on the road, save money, help the environment, and improve your quality of life. A few examples:

· Instead of making separate trips for every errand, plan trips that allow you to check off at least three boxes on your to-do list.

- Instead of driving to the supermarket every two or three days, purchase enough groceries to last a week.
- For holidays, explore natural and cultural wonders that are closer to home. While the 100-mile diet is a hot trend, the 100-mile holiday might be next.
- Take one long vacation instead of a series of shorter holidays. Spending two consecutive weeks at a cottage or ski resort instead of seven weekends would reduce your travel distance and travel time by 86%.

### Public Transit

Public transit is a much more pro-environmental choice than driving, unless you are the only person on the bus or train. A standard diesel bus gets approximately 2 kilometers (5 miles) per gallon, but with 40 passengers aboard, a bus gets 80 passenger kilometers per liter. Hybrid diesel buses, already in production and use, increase fuel efficiency by up to 60%, dramatically cutting greenhouse gas emissions and other forms of air pollution. By using public transit you reduce congestion, reduce the risk of accidents, and save money. Tax incentives for transit users are common in Canada and the U.S., making your savings even greater. From a broader economic perspective, public investment in transit creates more jobs and more economic activity than investment in road building.

Consider the following tips for public transit users:

- Learn your options—what services are offered and how close to your home?
- Check the schedule—a few minutes invested in consulting schedules can save many minutes of waiting. Keep checking, as schedules change frequently.
- Ask the driver for help—most transit employees are generous with advice on making your trip as easy as possible.
- Enjoy the ride—with someone else driving, you can read, listen to music, knit, or sit back and enjoy the scenery.

## Car Sharing

Car-sharing organizations enable members to have access to vehicles when needed while saving money, reducing the hassles of vehicle ownership (purchasing, insuring, repairing, parking, etc.), and reducing environmental impacts. In general, you gain access to a fleet of strategically located vehicles in exchange for a one-time refundable membership fee, a monthly rate, and an hourly or mileage rate. Members of car-sharing organizations own fewer cars, walk, cycle, and rollerblade more often, take more trips on public transit, drive less frequently, and travel shorter distances. Society also benefits from car sharing. Older cars are replaced with new vehicles that pollute less. More green space can be protected, as fewer parking spaces are required. There is less traffic congestion, fewer accidents, fewer greenhouse gas emissions, and less air pollution.

The popularity of car sharing is accelerating in Australia and the U.K. More than one hundred and fifty thousand North Americans already belong to car-sharing programs, using approximately five thousand vehicles. Each car-sharing vehicle can replace five to twenty privately owned vehicles. Car-sharing users reduce their average annual vehicle kilometers by 39% to 54%. As with cycling and walking, car-sharing members consistently report increased satisfaction with their quality of life. To find out more about car sharing in the U.S., see www.carsharing.net. In Australia, see www.travelsmart.gov.au/links/index.html. In Canada, see www.carsharing.ca.

## Carpooling

Carpooling is similar to car sharing but usually involves shared use of a privately owned vehicle (e.g., your car or a friend's van) on trips to shared destinations. Many jurisdictions encourage carpooling by offering tax breaks, free parking, and access to high-occupancy vehicle lanes. By carpooling, you can cut your operating costs from 50% to 75% and reduce your transportation footprint by the same amount. There are extensive carpooling resources on the Internet. In Australia, see www.travel smart. gov.au/links/index.html. In North America, see www.rideshare.us, www.erideshare.com, www.carpooltool.com, www.carpoolworld.com, www.ridester.com, and www.rideshare-directory.com. In the U.K., see www.nationalcarshare.co.uk.

### Scooters and Electric Bicycles

Electric bicycles have rechargeable batteries and provide a little extra push when you are pedaling. While the magnitude of environmental benefits depends on the kind of energy used to generate the electricity for recharging, electric bicycles are a substantial improvement over cars. By contrast scooters have an environmental record that is mixed, even though they may look cool. Some scooters have two-stroke engines that are dirty and inefficient, meaning your scooter could be pumping out more pollution than a big SUV. Only scooters with four-stroke engines are environmentally friendly.

### Delivery Services

People make hundreds of shopping trips annually (mostly for groceries). If you live in a city and usually drive to the supermarket, you can reduce the transportation portion of your ecological footprint by having groceries delivered to your home. One truck can deliver the week's groceries to dozens of families, preventing many trips to the supermarket and saving you some valuable time. Home delivery can reduce fuel consumption and greenhouse gas emissions by up to 70%.

### Videoconferencing

Videoconferencing is an increasingly effective and affordable option, enabling you to avoid extensive travel for meetings, presentations, and conferences. The time that you would otherwise waste traveling can be used more productively, whether at work or at play.

## *Telecommuting*

Telecommuting means working full-time or part-time at home and staying in touch by phone or email. The average number of daily trips taken on telecommuting days is anywhere from 27% to 51% less than on non-telecommuting days, and vehicle kilometers traveled are 53% to 77% less. Thus telecommuting can save you valuable time and money, decrease stress, reduce your household's need for a second car, and lead directly to significant reductions in emissions of harmful air pollutants.

· · · · · · · · · · · · · · · · · · · · · · · · · · · · · · · · · · · · · · · · · · · · · · · · · · ·

## ≋ PLANES, TRAINS, AND BOATS ≋

AIR TRAVEL increased fivefold from 1970 to 2000, and carbon dioxide emissions from aviation are expected to triple by 2050. Although some new aircraft are more fuel-efficient than their predecessors, and today's flights have fewer empty seats, the inescapable fact is that flying generates a high volume of greenhouse gas emissions per passenger kilometer. Direct flights are slightly better than flights with extra stops. However, as George Monbiot concluded in his book *Heat* after exhaustively examining all of the alternatives, the only way to substantially reduce your impact from flying is to fly less.

Are ships a better choice for long distance travel? No. Ships traveling internationally are major sources of air pollution, water pollution, and greenhouse gas emissions.

What about trains? In general, trains produce fewer greenhouse gas emissions per passenger kilometer than airplanes. In Europe, trains are a popular, effective, and environmentally friendly alternative to flying. In North America, passenger rail systems have been neglected for many decades, resulting in a legacy of underwhelming service. Public policy changes and major investments are needed to make long-distance rail a more attractive and affordable option in the U.S. and Canada. In Australia, trains offer a scenic and relaxing alternative to flying or driving on some long routes, such as Perth to Sydney or Adelaide to Darwin.

Reducing your driving and flying could provide huge safety, health, environmental, financial, and social benefits. The world would be a safer place to live if more people chose alternatives to driving. The latest data from Canada and the U.S. show that every year almost fifty thousand people die and 3 million more are injured in vehicle crashes. That's more than one hundred and thirty deaths per day. Based on current statistics, almost every American will be injured in a motor vehicle accident at some point in his or her lifetime. According to the U.S. National Safety Council, buses and trains are at least twenty times safer than cars.

The world would be a much healthier place if people racked up fewer road and air kilometers. Among the negative health outcomes caused by vehicle pollution are premature death, cancer, respiratory illness, cardiovascular disease, damage to the nervous system, and adverse effects on reproduction and fetal development. Air pollution contributes to the death of at least ten thousand Canadians annually. More than 136 million Americans live in areas with unacceptable air pollution. Children living near freeways suffer deficits in lung function and an 89% higher risk of asthma than children living farther away from busy roads. The health risks caused by vehicle exhaust are borne not only by people spending time outside but also by drivers and passengers. For example, children riding in diesel school buses are exposed to high levels of air pollution while inside the bus.

Actions that decrease vehicle use also decrease the world's unhealthy and expensive dependence on imported oil. In the U.S., transportation consumes seven out of ten barrels of oil used. Americans spend almost a million dollars per minute to purchase oil, the majority of which is imported.

Reducing your road kilometers will save you a bundle of money. Owning and operating a car in the U.S., Canada, or Australia costs between $8,000 and $13,000 annually (not including tolls and parking). In the U.K., driving costs are even higher. These estimates include only direct expenses such as gas, insurance, repairs, and car payments. A more comprehensive assessment would include the environmental and social costs of pollution, accidents, and congestion. In the U.S., these external costs are estimated to be as high as sixty-seven cents per mile. A few cents per mile sounds insignificant until you consider the trillions of miles traveled. Then the costs add up to between $400 billion and $2 trillion dollars per year. These gigantic dollar figures do not include the military costs of protecting and securing oil supplies. Finally, gas prices have tripled since 1998 and are continuing to soar, as global demand increases and supplies are steady or declining.

Commuting by means other than your car may actually be faster in some congested urban areas. Average vehicle speeds in cities have been declining 5% per decade. Canadians spend sixty-three minutes a day commuting, an increase of 17% from 1992 because of longer trips and more traffic congestion. The average Canadian spends the equivalent of thirty-four eight-hour days a year driving to and from work. In 2003, drivers in America's eighty-five most congested urban areas experienced 3.7 billion hours of travel delay and wasted 2.3 billion gallons of fuel, costing a total of $63 billion. In Australia, commuting costs more than $20 billion a year, and 10% of working parents spend more time commuting than caring for their children. British workers endure the longest average commute in Europe—ninety-two minutes a day.

### Inspiration

London, England, was suffering from severe gridlock, with average traffic speeds as slow as 10 kilometers (6 miles) per hour, until Mayor Ken Livingstone imposed a congestion tax on vehicles entering the city center in 2003. The tax is a success. About fifty thousand fewer vehicles are entering the city center daily, with people switching to public transit, cycling, walking, and carpooling. Traffic speeds have increased, transit service is faster and more reliable, accidents have been reduced, noise and pollution levels are down, and the city has a new source of revenue for investing in sustainable transportation. The tax initially generated vocal opposition but is now accepted and being copied in other large cities.

The ecological footprint of a vehicle is dominated by its fuel use. Although Model T Fords used 7.8 liters of fuel per 100 kilometers (30 miles per gallon) as early as 1908, the average fuel efficiency of motor vehicles in Canada and the U.S. today is actually worse. The fuel economy of the American vehicle fleet is at its lowest point in twenty years at 14 liters per 100 kilometers (16.7 miles per gallon). In part, this backsliding is due to exploding sales of light-duty trucks (SUVs, pickups, and minivans). In 1976, four cars were sold per truck or van. In 2002, for the first time, more SUVs, trucks, and vans were sold than cars in the U.S. A recent review of motor vehicle technology concluded, "in terms of environmental efficiency, today's automobile is in its infancy."

Against this dark backdrop, we can set three pieces of good news. First, there are revolutionary zero emission vehicles on the horizon (as previewed in Chapter 1). Second, not all vehicles being manufactured today are gas guzzlers. Reasonably fuel-efficient cars for sale today include hybrids, diesel vehicles, specialized electric cars, and some conventional vehicles. Third, in 2007 the Toyota Prius became the first hybrid to crack the top-ten list in American monthly vehicle sales.

### Hybrids

Hybrid vehicles have both internal combustion engines and electric motors. Hybrids are easy to drive and offer better mileage, greater range, and lower fuel costs than conventional vehicles, while producing fewer greenhouse gases and less air pollution. Retail prices are higher than for regular vehicles, but hybrid prices should fall over time and rising gas prices should make them more competitive economically. For example, given the average distance traveled and recent high gas prices of more than $1 a liter ($3 a gallon) in the U.S., a Toyota Prius would save several tons of carbon dioxide and almost $1,500 in gas expenses annually compared with a regular vehicle. Hybrids may also qualify for federal, state, provincial, and employer rebates, free or reduced parking fees, and reduced insurance costs. The widespread adoption of hybrid vehicles by taxi fleets in North America reflects their reliability, efficiency, and low operating costs.

Even more promising than regular hybrid vehicles are plug-in hybrids, which have a larger electric motor, smaller gas engine, more battery storage, and can be recharged by plugging a cord into ordinary power outlets. Plug-in hybrids could get at least 2.3 liters per 100 kilometers (100 miles per gallon) and could operate as zero emission vehicles in cities (i.e., for trips of up to 65 kilometers). The catch with any kind of electric transportation, including plug-in hybrids, is the type of energy used to produce the electricity. Plug-in hybrids are not yet for sale, although prototypes are being road tested.

### Electric Vehicles

Electric vehicles produce no local emissions during their operation, making them desirable in urban areas. Currently, however, high cost, short range, and long recharging times limit their viability for many people. A good example of the type of electric vehicles on sale today is the ZENN (zero emissions, no noise). The ZENN has a range of 56 kilometers (35 miles), a maximum speed of 40 kilometers (25 miles) per hour, and takes eight or nine hours to recharge. This type of vehicle may be useful in some urban settings or as a second car. Ironically, more versatile full-sized electric vehicles were made in the 1990s but have been discontinued. The most notorious example is General Motors' EV-1, subject of the film *Who Killed the Electric Car?* The degree to which an electric vehicle is environmentally friendly depends largely on the source of the electricity used for recharging the batteries. An electric car in France is nuclear powered, in Quebec or British Columbia it is powered by hydroelectricity, and in many parts of Australia, Canada, and the U.S. it is powered by coal. A key to the future success of electric vehicle technology involves improving battery performance.

## Diesels

Diesel vehicles produce lower carbon dioxide emissions than gasoline vehicles. However, while new models of diesel vehicles are much cleaner than previous models, they still produce more health-harming air pollutants—sulfur oxides, nitrogen oxides, and fine particulate matter. In the U.K., aggressive climate change policies encouraging the purchase of diesel vehicles led to estimated reductions of 400,000 tons of carbon dioxide and 1 million barrels of oil annually. Unfortunately, these policies predated the introduction of cleaner diesel vehicles, so that air pollution from the additional diesels also resulted in an estimated ninety deaths annually.

## Buying a Cleaner Car

The greenest choice is not owning a motor vehicle. If you genuinely need to own your own vehicle, strive to purchase one that meets your needs while offering the highest possible fuel economy rating. According to scientists at the Massachusetts Institute of Technology, hybrids are the most environmentally friendly choice, providing a 37% to 47% decrease in lifecycle energy use and carbon dioxide emissions compared with conventional vehicles. Hybrids are increasingly available throughout the full range of vehicle classes, including not only passenger cars but also SUVs and pickup trucks. If financial constraints make the initial premium of purchasing hybrids unaffordable, there are less expensive conventional cars that still achieve relatively high fuel efficiency ratings. The American Council for an Energy Efficient Economy maintains an excellent green car website (www.greenercars.com). Governments also provide current information on fuel efficiency. Vehicles with the best fuel economy in North America in 2007 were the Toyota Prius, the Honda Civic Hybrid, and the Toyota Camry Hybrid. You can find out more about fuel economy for specific vehicles on the Internet. In the U.S., see www.fueleconomy.gov/feg/bestworst.shtml. In Canada, see http://oee1.nrcan.gc.ca. In Australia, see www.greenvehicleguide.gov.au. In the U.K., see www.vcacarfueldata.org.uk.

Replacing your current vehicle with a hybrid can reduce the transportation component of your ecological footprint by 50% (if you switch from a conventional sedan to a hybrid sedan) to 75% (if you switch from an SUV to a hybrid sedan). Consider delaying the purchase of diesel vehicles until tough new pollution standards are in force (2009 in the U.S., later in Canada). If your needs can be met by a fully electric vehicle despite the limited range of this technology today, and if your electricity is green, then you can reduce your transport footprint by 90%. Getting rid of your household's second, third, and fourth cars will also reduce your footprint. Finally, if you are driving a car that is more than fifteen years old, it's time to retire it. It probably causes two or three times as much air pollution as a current model. Programs throughout the industrialized world offer incentives for scrapping your old vehicle, ranging from free transit passes to rebates on the purchase of bikes and cleaner vehicles. In Canada, see www.carheaven.ca and www.scrapit.ca. In the U.S., see www.arb.ca.gov/msprog/avrp/avrp.htm. In the U.K., see www.scrapcar.co.uk.

### IMPROVE YOUR DRIVING HABITS

As well as driving less frequently and operating a greener vehicle or joining a car-sharing organization, you should consider the way you drive. Aggressive driving is a dangerous habit that saves a minimal amount of time (2.5 minutes per hour of driving), yet uses 37% more fuel and creates more toxic emissions. A far safer and more planet-friendly approach is eco-driving: driving habits that reduce fuel consumption, carbon dioxide emissions, air pollution, noise, vehicle repair and maintenance costs, driver and passenger stress, and accident rates. In Europe, eco-driving courses are rapidly gaining popularity. Eco-driving is now part of the driver education curriculum in Germany, the Netherlands, and the U.K. Adoption of eco-driving throughout the industrialized world would reduce fuel consumption by at least 10%, saving billions of liters of fuel and millions of tons of carbon dioxide emissions annually.

Consider the following eco-driving tips:

- Drive less—walk, cycle, use public transit, combine trips, work at home, car share, carpool, use videoconferences, and telecommute.
- Turn off the air conditioning and other energy consuming devices.
- Slow down—it's safer and saves fuel.
- Start gradually and anticipate stops—rapid acceleration and braking waste gas, increase pollution, and wear out your brakes.
- Keep your tires inflated to the recommended pressure. Underinflated tires cost Canadian light-duty vehicle owners almost 643 million liters (141 million gallons) of fuel annually.
- Maximize aerodynamics (remove roof racks, bike racks, and so on when not using them).
- Travel light—an extra 45 kilograms (100 pounds) in your trunk reduces fuel economy by 1% to 2%.
- Avoid idling, which gets zero kilometers per liter.
- Avoid rush hour. Stop-and-go driving burns more gas and increases emissions of smog-forming pollutants.
- Avoid high-octane gasoline, which takes more energy to produce, contains additional toxic substances, and provides few if any benefits.

### SWITCH TO CLEANER FUELS

Because of climate change, concerns about running out of oil, and rising gas prices, there is growing interest in alternative fuels. Potential substitutes for gasoline include hydrogen, liquefied petroleum gas, compressed natural gas, and biofuels.

### Hydrogen

Hydrogen is hyped as the fuel of the future because it can be used in fuel cell vehicles, producing only water and heat as by-products. Like electricity, hydrogen is an energy carrier rather than an energy source like gasoline. The environmental pedigree of hydrogen depends on how it's produced—whether from fossil fuels or renewable energy sources. Despite the construction of so-called hydrogen highways in California and British Columbia, there are few vehicles built to run on hydrogen and even fewer filling stations. There are unresolved concerns about cost, storage, performance, and infrastructure. However, even critics of hydrogen admit that continued research and development in hydrogen and transportation fuel cell technologies remains important because of their potential.

### Liquified Petroleum Gas and Compressed Natural Gas

LPG (liquefied petroleum gas, or propane) and CNG (compressed natural gas) offer modest reductions in smog-forming air emissions and carbon dioxide emissions, and are less expensive than gasoline. LPG and CNG vehicles are not produced commercially in large numbers, but conventional vehicles can be retrofitted to run on these fuels. A significant problem is that CNG and LPG are less widely available than gasoline and diesel. Dual-fuel vehicles use LPG or CNG when available, but can also run on gasoline.

### Biofuels

Biofuels (biodiesel and ethanol) represent a form of renewal energy that can be produced from various kinds of agricultural products and wood waste. The environmental virtues of biofuels depend largely on the fuel source and where it comes from. Biodiesel is produced from vegetable oils, animal fats, or recycled restaurant grease. Using biodiesel as a full or partial substitute for diesel can substantially reduce emissions of air pollution and greenhouse gases, with only modest reductions in performance. Biodiesel blended with diesel at up to 5% can be used in any diesel vehicle while higher blends may require minor engine modifications. Biodiesel made from canola may be a green option but biodiesel from palm oil plantations that replaced native tropical forests is definitely not.

Ethanol made from grains is the most widely used alternative fuel today. Ethanol can be blended with gasoline (up to 10%, or E10) and used in all vehicles made after 1977, while higher levels of ethanol (up to 85%, or E85) can be used in special flex-fuel vehicles. There is a heated debate about whether ethanol's environmental benefits outweigh its costs. Again, the fuel crop and growing location will determine the eco-friendliness. Corn-based ethanol offers the fewest benefits.

There is one more catch and one more reason for optimism regarding biofuels. The catch is that producing biofuels from crops on a large scale would require huge areas of land, displacing food production and driving up prices. The optimism is derived from the fact that ethanol can be made from cellulose (straw, agricultural waste, wood), which provides much greater environmental benefits than ethanol from grains. Cellulosic ethanol can provide 70% to 90% lower greenhouse gas emissions over its life cycle compared to gasoline but is not yet commercially available.

You may achieve modest reductions in the transportation component of your ecological footprint by using renewable fuels like biodiesel (in diesel vehicles) and ethanol (in regular vehicles), but because of concerns about displacing food crops, today's biofuels can make only a limited contribution to more sustainable transport.

### CARBON CREDITS

Many people, despite their environmental concerns, will continue to drive and fly, even if they reduce the frequency and distance of such trips. One approach to offsetting the effect of driving and flying on climate change involves voluntarily purchasing carbon credits (also called offsets). The price you pay depends on the distance you travel and your mode of transport. Organizations selling carbon credits invest your money (or at least some portion of it) in renewable energy projects, energy efficiency projects, or planting trees. From the Rolling Stones to the International Olympic Committee, individuals, corporations, and entire cities are purchasing credits to offset their carbon dioxide emissions. The Canadian airline WestJet will even pay for your carbon credits if you book flights through an organization called Offsetters (www.offsetters.ca).

Concerns have been raised about the effectiveness of many carbon credit operations. The concept is still new, is unregulated, and there is a wide range of quality in the credits available. Tree planting was popular in the early days of the concept but its credibility is now being questioned. Independent assessments have recommended the following suppliers of carbon credits:

- Atmosfair (www.atmosfair.de).
- Climate Friendly (www.climatefriendly.com).
- Climate Trust (www.climatetrust.org).
- myclimate (www.myclimate.org).
- NativeEnergy (www.nativeenergy.com).

### RECAP

A century ago, transportation underwent rapid and radical changes as cars replaced horses. A similar transformation is required today. Clean, safe, healthy, attractive cities and a stable climate need to become our top transportation priorities. Some governments and industries see technology as a silver bullet. They're wrong. Green technology can't solve all the problems caused by our current transport system. Cleaner cars don't address congestion, accidents, urban sprawl, or impacts on biodiversity. A genuinely sustainable transportation system requires transforming land-use patterns and moving to renewable energy. These changes will take decades, so we need to start now.

You can contribute to the evolution of a greener transport system by choosing your home's location wisely, driving and flying less, and using human-powered travel, public transit, car sharing, carpooling, telecommuting, and videoconferencing. According to the experts on human happiness, you'll be delighted by the freedom of leaving your car behind. If you have to own a vehicle, buy the most fuel-efficient model you can afford, practice eco-driving, and fill'er up with relatively clean fuel. All of these choices are available today, and your support will help them grow.

# 5

# Less Stuff:
# The Zero Waste Challenge

*one word to you, to*
*you and your children:*
*stay together,*
*learn the flowers,*
*go light.*

GARY SNYDER

❧   ❧   ❧

S hopping and watching television are replacing baseball and hockey as
the national pastimes of the U.S. and Canada. On a daily basis, the
average American spends more time shopping than participating in
religious and spiritual activities, or sports and recreation. Watching television takes up more time than housework, education, sports, exercise, raising children, volunteering, cooking, and cleaning combined. Canadians
spend a similar amount of time shopping but watch less television. Commercials on TV and in other media relentlessly tell us to buy, buy, buy.

Everything we buy has a hidden history of environmental impacts,
beginning in places as disparate as forests, fields, oceans, laboratories,
and open pit mines. Many finished products bear little relationship to
their initial raw state or area of origin. Processed food expunges any

reminder that all of our nutrition was once alive. Recent books reveal the strange and often disturbing life stories of everything from T-shirts to Twinkies.

A T-shirt may have its roots in a Texas cotton field that's been drenched in pesticides and irrigated with water from the disappearing Ogallala aquifer. After being harvested by migrant workers, the cotton is shipped across the Pacific Ocean to a textile mill in China. Then the T-shirt travels back across the Pacific, destined for a store in the U.S. The shirt is worn for a few months, maybe years, then sent to the dump or dropped in a charity's collection box. From there it's trucked to a textile recycling facility. Used T-shirts may be sold in vintage clothing stores, turned into rags, or sent across the Atlantic to bustling markets in Africa. Every step of the journey is fueled by oil—for agriculture, trucking, and shipping—and every step produces pollution.

The T-shirt illustrates how economies consume raw materials and excrete waste and pollution in order to produce goods and services. The American economy uses more than 85,000 kilograms (187,000 pounds) of natural resources per person each year, not including water. In other words, for every American, the economy chews up three times an average person's body weight in resources every single day. That's the consumption side. On the waste side, Americans generate 86,000 kilograms (189,200 pounds) of waste and pollution per person annually. The atmosphere is by far the biggest dumping ground, with carbon dioxide, the main culprit in changing the Earth's climate, making up more than 80% of the waste stream.

As William McDonough and Michael Braungart observe in their book *Cradle to Cradle*, "what most people see in their garbage cans is just the tip of a material iceberg." When we use paper, we're blind to the damage wrought on forests, the logging roads built, the wood wasted, and the energy and resources used to build, operate, and maintain chainsaws, feller-bunchers, grapple-yarders, logging trucks, and pulp and paper mills. When we eat a meal, we rarely consider soil erosion, the oil used to make pesticides and fertilizers, or the energy and resources used to manufacture, operate, and maintain tractors, trucks, and refrigeration units, distribution centers, and grocery stores. When we turn on the TV, we seldom think of mountains being razed to mine coal, streams and valleys destroyed by overburden removed to get at the coal, the energy and resources needed to build, operate, and maintain coal-fired power plants, or the mercury, sulfur dioxide, and carbon dioxide that power plants spew into the atmosphere. Our consumption is completely disconnected from its environmental origins and consequences.

Understanding the connections between our individual actions and the broader environmental consequences generated by the economy gives us a compelling incentive to reduce our consumption. We can turn the daunting statistics about resource use and pollution upside down by reducing our demand and sending tsunami-like ripples along the entire supply chain. By reducing your consumption of goods by 1 kilogram, you can save approximately 200 kilograms (440 pounds) of natural resources and prevent 200 kilograms of waste and pollution. By this measure, individual acts of conservation can have a huge effect.

Experts believe that wealthy industrialized nations must reduce consumption of energy and resources by 90% for the planet to survive the double whammy of population growth and rising affluence. Reducing resource use to one-tenth of previous levels may sound like a radical idea, but it's not. The highly regarded Organization for Economic Co-operation and Development (OECD), whose thirty members include Canada, the U.S., Australia, the U.K., and most of the world's wealthiest nations, agrees that a 90% reduction in the use of natural resources is needed. The OECD even argues that it is "relatively easy" to achieve a 75% reduction in resource use and environmental impact. The World Resources Institute, the Wuppertal Institute, and the David Suzuki Foundation also endorse the 90% goal. The scale of action needed means everyone has a vital role to play.

In Chapter 1 we described the growing number of governments and corporations that are striving to achieve zero waste, meaning that nothing will have to be sent to dumps or incinerated. Zero waste is also a great goal for individuals and families because it changes your perspective on every product you buy, making you think about where things will end up. Some people view zero waste as a real target, while others view it as more of an ideal. In either case, it's worth trying to achieve it. In fact, some enterprising individuals have already succeeded in diverting 95% or more of their waste from the dump by carefully screening the things they buy, reducing consumption of particular items, composting, and recycling.

## Inspiration

Dick and Jeanne Roy are an all-American couple. Dick Roy was president of his class at Oregon State University, an officer in the navy, and a corporate lawyer with a prestigious law firm in Portland. Jeanne worked as an activist on air quality and solid waste issues, contributing to the development of Portland's excellent recycling programs. In 1993, the Roys started the Northwest Earth Institute, an organization devoted to helping people move towards sustainable lifestyles. In an entire year, the Roys produce one regular sized can of garbage.

Colin Beavan, better known as No Impact Man, lives in New York City with his wife, daughter, and dog. No Impact Man has garnered international attention for his effort to minimize his ecological footprint. Beavan and his family buy nothing new, use no fossil-fuel-powered transportation, eat only local food, and use no packaging or plastic. Recognizing that having absolutely no impact defies the laws of physics, they are attempting to offset their negative environmental impacts with positive actions, including planting trees, cleaning up beaches, and composting.

## WHAT YOU CAN DO

We've already addressed the three categories that contribute to 80% of the ecological footprint of people living in industrialized countries— housing, food, and transport. As for the remaining 20% of your footprint, there are countless products and activities that contribute but none that make up a particularly large slice of the pie. A single Wal-Mart store carries more than one hundred thousand different products. Going through each possible category would make this book so long it would take up an environmentally disastrous number of pages and be unreadable. As well, because products change so quickly and so many new businesses, goods, and services enter the market every year, specific advice tends to become out of date quickly.

Instead, we recommend six general ways you can move towards achieving zero waste:

1. Following principles of sustainable consumption.
2. Reducing your consumption.
3. Reusing items when possible.
4. Repairing items when possible.
5. Recycling when possible.
6. Composting your kitchen, lawn, and garden waste.

## TWELVE GUIDING PRINCIPLES
## OF SUSTAINABLE CONSUMPTION

1. Remember the big picture. Spend less time worrying about plastic bags and disposable cups and more time thinking about where you live, energy use in your home, how often and how far you drive (and fly), and what you eat.
2. Don't buy stuff that you don't need. Among the three environmental commandments—reduce, reuse, and recycle—reduce is by far the most important. It is obvious that the planet cannot sustain 6.6 billion people consuming at the rate of North Americans or Australians, let alone the 9 billion people expected to be here by 2050.
3. Make food, not waste. Before you buy something, think ahead to when you'll stop using it. Every product, when you're finished with it, should be food for either the biological economy (readily biodegradable materials) or the industrial economy (recyclable or reusable raw materials for new products). If a product is a combination of both, then it should be capable of being easily separated or disassembled.

4. Buy local. The closer to home a product is grown, built, or made, generally the lower the transportation costs and associated pollution. You can also have greater confidence that local production methods will be safe for human health and the environment, as suggested by the spate of recent problems with imports from China.

5. Go for quality, not quantity. Select durable products and maximize their reuse through regular maintenance and care. Keep products such as clothing, sporting equipment, and kitchen goods in circulation through thrift stores and charities. Choose products certified as ecologically and socially responsible by an independent organization. (See "Certification," below.)

6. Support renewable energy. Seek out products and businesses that rely on wind, solar, geothermal, or other renewable sources of power.

7. Make healthy choices. Avoid purchasing or using toxic and hazardous products. Sometimes the danger is obvious—the product's label says "Warning," "Poison," "Toxic," "Flammable," or "Explosive." In the absence of these warning signs, watch out for long chemical names in the list of ingredients on a product. Chemicals that you never heard of or can't pronounce are prime candidates for suspicion about negative health and environmental effects. (See "Label-reading 101," below.)

8. Look for a high proportion of recycled content. To fulfill the promise of recycling requires people to purchase recycled products. Sometimes you do this unintentionally, like when you buy aluminum cans or appliances made with recycled steel. Other times, the onus is on you to seek out products made from recycled materials, such as school or office supplies.

9. Demand better options. Green choices should be easy to find and affordable, but misguided laws and policies often favor unsustainable products. Individual actions can only go so far, and need to be complemented by strong, pro-environment public policies. The more people vote for environmentally informed candidates, speak up on behalf of innovative green solutions, and push for change, the sooner the shift towards a sustainable future will come about. (See Chapter 6, Citizen Green.)

10. Encourage environmental leaders and innovators. Eco-entrepreneurs and green companies often face competitive disadvantages because quality materials and clean products have higher prices (even if their long-term or overall costs are lower). Be a leader yourself and give them your support.

11. Clean up your mental environment. To start reducing the constant stream of commercial messages urging you to buy more stuff, try watching less television, canceling subscriptions to catalogs, and limiting your Internet use. Protecting children is especially vital. Between 1980 and 2004, the amount spent on advertising that directly targets American children rose from $100 million per year to $15 billion. Children now see an average of forty thousand television commercials per year. Push your government to copy Sweden, the U.K., and Quebec, where certain types of advertising aimed at kids are prohibited.

12. Trade money for time. This may be the best deal you ever make, the personal equivalent of the U.S. buying Alaska from Russia for $7.2 million in 1867 (less than two cents per acre). People in Canada and the U.S. feel more stressed than ever before, and bemoan the fact that there's so little free time in their lives. This isn't surprising, considering the fact that Americans work about 350 hours per year (ten weeks) more than Europeans.

In addition, do what you can to avoid using high-impact products (including gasoline-powered lawnmowers, leafblowers, and snowblowers; tobacco; pesticides and fertilizers; and hazardous cleaners and paints). And if possible, don't participate in high-impact activities:

- Powerboating
- Jet skiing
- Snowmobiling
- Recreational off-road driving
- Fishing
- Golfing

By avoiding high-impact products and activities, and by following principles of sustainable consumption, you'll be able to progress towards the goal of zero waste. These principles apply to just about every imaginable category of goods and services that you may contemplate purchasing—clothing, carpets, toys, furniture, paint, cleaners, appliances, electronics, cosmetics, sporting equipment. Take clothing as an example. Applying the twelve guiding principles means thinking about whether you really need more T-shirts or shoes, checking out vintage (second-hand) clothing stores, focusing on natural (and ideally organic) fibers such as wool, hemp, bamboo (you'll be amazed how soft it is), Tencel (made from the cellulose in wood pulp), and cotton, striving to buy from local designers and producers, and reducing clutter by donating your used clothing to charities.

## LABEL-READING 101

SINCE GREEN is the new black, it's trendy for manufacturers and retailers to claim that their products are environmentally friendly. How do you know if their claims are accurate or if they're greenwash? First, check for certification by a respected organization. Second, be skeptical about vague claims. Words such as "natural," "green," and "safe" can mean just about anything and are widely misused. Third, look for specific details. The three green arrows symbol and the word "recycle" or "recyclable" mean that a product is recyclable but not that it is made of recycled content. If the label says "recycled," look for how much of the content is recycled. There's a big difference between 5% and 100%. Fourth, context is important. A "recyclable" product won't be recycled unless it's included in your community program. A "biodegradable" product will not biodegrade if you put it in the garbage, since even food and paper may not break down in landfills. You can get full details on all of the various claims made on product labels from Consumer Reports at www.greener choices.org.

# CERTIFICATION—A HELPFUL INDICATOR OF SUSTAINABILITY

One of the most reliable signs that a product is genuinely green is certification. The following programs are among the most widely respected.

### CORPORATE STANDARD OF COMPASSION FOR ANIMALS

The Coalition for Consumer Information on Cosmetics certifies cosmetics, personal care products (e.g., shampoo), and household products (e.g., laundry detergent) that are not tested on animals. See www.leapingbunny.org.

### CRADLE-TO-CRADLE CERTIFICATION

Cradle-to-cradle certification (c2c) sets a high standard for "environmentally intelligent" design, examining the entire life cycle of environmentally safe and healthy materials. See www.c2ccertified.com.

### ENERGY STAR

The Energy Star rating system used in North America, Europe, Australia, and elsewhere rewards products that use substantially less energy than comparable products, and currently applies to more than fifty categories of products including appliances, windows, air conditioners, furnaces, thermostats, fans, sky lights, roofing, lighting, and new houses. See www.energystar.gov, www.energystar.gc.ca, www.en-energystar.org, and www.energystar.gov.au.

### ENVIRONMENTAL CHOICE

Canada's Environmental Choice logo certifies products and services as environmentally responsible based on life cycle analysis of harmful emissions, recycled content, water use, energy efficiency, and other factors. See www.environmentalchoice.ca.

### EUROPEN ECO-LABEL

The Eco-label flower is used throughout the European Union to identify goods and services that meet strict scientific criteria for minimizing environmental impacts. See http://ec.europa.eu/environment/ecolabel/index_en.htm.

### FOREST STEWARDSHIP COUNCIL

The Forest Stewardship Council (FSC) sets standards for responsible forest management and certifies wood and paper products. See www.fsc.org.

### GOOD ENVIRONMENTAL CHOICE

Australia's independent Environmental Choice label identifies products and services that have a smaller ecological footprint than their competitors. See www.aela.org.au.

### GREEN GUARD

The Green Guard Environmental Institute certifies low-emission building materials and indoor products. See www.greenguard.org.

### GREEN SEAL

Green Seal certifies paints, adhesives, and cleaning products. See www.greenseal.org.

### GREENSPEC

GreenSpec certifies a wide range of building, renovation, and home furnishing products. See the Materials Directory at www.buildinggreen.com.

### SCIENTIFIC CERTIFICATION SYSTEMS (SCS)

SCS certifies food, flowers, fish, electricity, wood products, and manufactured goods for various levels of environmental performance. Their Indoor Advantage certification program guarantees that products used indoors have minimal or no volatile organic carbon emissions. See www.scscertified.com.

For decades, environmentalists have called for reduced consumption of energy and resources, a rallying cry widely misconstrued as favoring a return to pre-industrial ways of life. In reality, what's needed is more efficient and responsible use of resources, a path towards a more advanced lifestyle being pioneered with enviable success by some of the greenest European nations. Those people who are unconvinced about the imperative to reduce should visit their local dump. It's an eye-opening experience. Of course the phrase "local dump" is a misnomer for many cities. Trash from Toronto, Ontario, is trucked across the border to Michigan and garbage from New York City goes to Pennsylvania. Rubbish from London in the U.K. is transported down the Thames River to landfills in Essex. And garbage from Sydney, Australia, travels 250 kilometers for dumping in an old open pit mine.

Americans, Australians, Britons, and Canadians generate similar amounts of garbage, placing their nations in the unenviable position of being world leaders in producing waste. Canadians generate about 420 kilograms (924 pounds) of household waste per person annually. In Canada and the U.K., about one-quarter of this total is recycled or composted. Despite the rise of recycling, the average person generates twice as much trash today as in 1960, and most of this trash could be recycled or composted. In the U.S., the main components of garbage are paper and cardboard (34% of the total weight) and food scraps and yard trimmings (25%). In other words, at least 60% of the waste being thrown away could be used as valuable resources.

There are many creative ways to reduce consumption without making sacrifices:

- Share goods. Share books, CDs, magazine subscriptions, and equipment that's used infrequently such as boats, hedge clippers, pruners, chain saws, or other power tools. You'll get to know your neighbors better, which generally contributes to increased happiness.
- Borrow instead of buying. Public libraries provide free (or very inexpen-

sive) books, and librarians often offer great suggestions. Most libraries also have a wide selection of DVDs, CDs, videotapes, and books on tape.

- Rent or lease instead of buying. This applies to a wide variety of products from video games to vehicles and appliances.
- Form an organic food buying co-op with a group of friends or colleagues. You'll save money and packaging by buying in bulk and reduce trips to the grocery store.
- Buy products that you have time to enjoy. For example, instead of subscribing to a daily newspaper, buy a newspaper only when you're actually going to read it, or read newspapers online or at the library.
- When choosing between similar products, select the one with the least unnecessary packaging. Also keep in mind that products in concentrated forms (e.g., laundry detergent, juice) reduce energy and resource use.

Taking advantage of new technologies can also reduce your ecological footprint. You can download music (legally) from the Internet instead of purchasing CDs. You can order books and DVDs from online sources and have them delivered through the mail. You can send e-birthday cards instead of paper cards. These services generally reduce energy use, air pollution, and greenhouse gas emissions.

### Inspiration

Plastic bags aren't just a waste of resources, they're dangerous. Plastic bags are made from oil. They do not biodegrade but rather photodegrade in the sun by breaking apart into small pieces of plastic dust, a process that takes up to one thousand years. It is estimated that in every square kilometer (0.38 square mile) of ocean there are over 18,000 pieces of plastic. Endangered sea turtles whose diet depends on eating jellyfish have been found dead from starvation. Autopsies revealed that their stomachs were plugged with plastic bags.

Some nations are responding to the blight of plastic bags by imposing a hefty fee for their use or even banning them altogether. Ireland placed a twenty-five-cent fee on plastic bags in 2002 and the use of plastic bags fell by roughly 90%. Irish Environment Minister Martin Cullen stated: "The levy has been an outstanding success in achieving what it set out to do. Over 1 billion plastic bags will be removed from circulation while raising funds for future environmentally friendly initiatives. It is clear that the levy has not only changed consumer behavior in relation to disposable plastic bags, it has also raised national consciousness about the role each one of us can and must play if we are to tackle collectively the problems of litter and waste management." Taiwan, Bangladesh, Rwanda, Mauritius, South Africa, San Francisco, and several Australian communities have outlawed some or all types of plastic bags.

## FAQS

*Grocery bags and coffee cups: Paper or plastic?* Neither. Studies comparing the environmental impacts of paper versus plastic produce conflicting results. One thing is clear—both, when used by the billions, have a substantial environmental impact. Instead, choose reusable bags and cups (ideally made from recycled/recyclable material).

*Diapers: Cloth or disposable?* Neither. A growing number of parents are practicing natural infant hygiene, which involves educating parents and babies to respond to cues so that infants become diaper-free at a very early age (www.natural-wisdom.com). Another eco-friendly option is the gDiaper, which consists of a cloth pant and snap-in liner with inserts made of wood pulp. The pants and liners are washed and reused and the inserts are flushed down the toilet. The gDiaper, certified as a cradle-to-cradle product, has the environmental edge because it sends no material to the landfill, uses no chlorine or plastics, and requires less washing (therefore, less water and energy usage) than regular cloth diapers (www.gdiapers.com).

Buying things that have been used before—such as clothing, sports equipment, books, and CDs—means that your purchase uses no new resources or energy. Everyday items you can reuse include:

- Stainless steel coffee mugs and chopsticks.
- Refillable containers.
- Cloth napkins and dishcloths.
- Paper (use both sides).
- Refillable printer cartridges.
- Rechargeable batteries. Rechargeable batteries can be reused up to one thousand times, replacing up to three hundred throwaway batteries and cutting way back on packaging.

Avoid disposable items such as paper napkins, plastic cutlery, cameras, batteries, and razors. Donate used clothing, toys, kitchen goods, and other household items to charities, thrift stores, or other organizations in need. These organizations typically take everything from clothes and textiles to appliances and furniture. All items should be clean and of reasonable quality. As an added incentive, donors of more valuable items can sometimes receive tax deductions.

Throughout the world, the Internet offers incredible opportunities for buying and selling (or better yet, giving away) used goods. Prominent examples include www.freecycle.org, www.Craigslist.org, www.throwplace.com, and www.ebay.com. You can also sell secondhand items the old-fashioned way at fairs, bazaars, swap meets, yard sales, and garage sales. You'll be amazed at the things people will buy.

### REPAIR

Repairing products is almost a lost art in this era of planned obsolescence. Think of the last time you saw a cobbler or a television repairman. Repairing products uses far fewer resources and generates far less waste than replacing them. If you regularly clean and service your appliances, computers, tools, clothes, shoes, and cars, they'll enjoy longer lives. Before you replace them, see if they can be repaired. The exceptions to the "repair 'em first" rule are gas-guzzling old cars, inefficient appliances, and water-sucking fixtures, which should be replaced with highly efficient products.

### RECYCLE

Perhaps no other environmental activity has caught the public imagination and become an ingrained part of life more quickly than recycling. In 1980 there was only one curbside recycling program in the entire U.S. By 2005 there were almost nine thousand. From 1990 to 1993 the rate of household recycling in Australia doubled, and the rates have continued to improve to this day. In Canada, 97% of the population claims to recycle at least some of the time, a dramatic rise in two decades. The benefits of recycling include saving energy, preventing greenhouse gas emissions, conserving natural resources for future generations, creating jobs, and providing valuable raw materials for industry. By recycling and composting, you can also lower your garbage collection bill (in communities that wisely charge by the bag). Although recycling is occasionally criticized as ineffective or as a waste of taxpayer's money, the evidence refutes these allegations. Studies show that recycling is clearly more environmentally responsible than incinerating or dumping waste.

In the U.S., the recycling industry processes more than 150 million tons of recyclable products and packaging into raw material for manufacturing every year. Recycling aluminum requires only 5% of the energy needed to produce aluminum from raw materials. Recycling appliances (most of the weight is steel) reduces mining waste by 97%, virgin material use by 90%, air pollution by 86%, water pollution by 76%, energy use by 74%, and water use by 40%. Recycling 1 ton of paper saves 17 trees, 359 liters (79 gallons) of oil, 31,780 liters (7,000 gallons) of water, and 2.5 cubic meters (3.3 cubic yards) of landfill space. Recycling a stack of newspapers just 1 meter high can save a tree.

The most commonly recycled products in the U.S. are:

- Lead-acid (car) batteries (99% recycling rate).
- Newspapers (89%).
- Corrugated boxes (72%).
- Major appliances (67%).
- Steel cans (63%).
- Aluminum beverage cans (45%).

Despite the rapid growth in the popularity of recycling, there is still a long way to go. The majority of the household waste going to landfills in many parts of the world could be recycled or composted. Americans throw away enough office paper each year to build a 3.6-meter-high wall from New York to Seattle, and dispose of enough aluminum in landfills to rebuild the entire commercial air fleet.

Most recycling programs accept metals, glass, paper, cardboard, and some plastics. Plastics are the hardest to recycle, providing another reason to avoid plastic containers and packaging. The most easily recycled plastics have the number 1 or 2 inside the recycling symbol (three arrows in a triangle), while numbers 3, 6, and 7 ought to be avoided when possible. Washing your recyclables helps protect the health of workers in the recycling industry and the value of the material.

Find out what your local recycling program accepts. Rules vary from community to community, so you will need to consult local government information sources or the Internet. In Australia, see www.recycling nearyou.com.au. In the U.K., see www.planetark.org/recycle_more_ uk.cfm. In the U.S., see www.nrc-recycle.org/localresources.aspx. In Canada, contact your provincial or local recycling organization for more information (e.g., in British Columbia www.rcbc.bc.ca/ and in Ontario www.rco.on.ca/).

Driving to a recycling center offsets some of the benefits of recycling, so make sure such trips are worthwhile. To reiterate, while recycling is important, reducing consumption is paramount.

Germany is a world leader in tackling the packaging problem. In the 1990s, Germany passed a law making manufacturers responsible for the packaging they produced. At the time, packaging waste was growing by 2% to 4% per year. Since that time, Germany has reduced the weight of packaging waste going to dumps or incinerators by almost 70%. Belgium, Sweden, and Austria subsequently passed similar laws and have achieved recycling rates of 65% to 75% for packaging. The German approach is now used throughout the European Union.

## COMPOST

Food scraps and yard trimmings make up about one-quarter of the trash in Canada and the U.S. Wherever you live, one of the most useful steps you can take to reduce the amount of trash you generate is to compost food scraps, yard trimmings, and even shredded paper. Composting is a natural biological process that converts organic material into a humus-like product (not to be confused with the delicious chickpea spread, hummus). In dumps, organic materials rot, releasing methane, a gas that contributes to climate change. Landfills produce up to 33% of North American methane.

By diverting organic materials from the dump, composting offers many benefits to you, your community, and the environment. You reduce the weight that garbage trucks need to carry, increase the lifespan of dumps, and lower methane emissions. Compost nourishes the soil and increases the number of healthy soil organisms such as worms and centipedes, simultaneously reducing the need for pesticides and artificial fertilizers. Children who watch their food scraps transformed into soil nutrients are filled with wonder at this natural process. In some communities, organic materials are picked up from your home along with other recyclables and taken to a central location for composting. These large-scale composting facilities then sell the final product to farmers and gardeners.

Contact your local government, as many offer discounted compost bins or worm farms. The Internet is a fertile source of information about all types of composting, as is a small book called *Home Composting Made Easy*. See www.compostguide.com, www.compost.org, www.epa.gov/compost, or www.cityfarmer.org/homecompost4.html.

Apartment dwellers can compost by practicing worm composting (vermi-composting). Worm composting uses red earthworms, also called redworms, to consume organic materials. The worms produce castings (an odor-free compost product used as mulch, soil conditioner, fertilizer, and topsoil additive). Naturally occurring organisms, such as bacteria, fungi, and millipedes, assist in breaking down the organic material. See www.compostguide.com/composting_worms.html.

About 25% of Canadian households compost their kitchen and/or lawn and garden waste, but the rate is as high as 90% in the provinces of Prince Edward Island and Nova Scotia. What explains this huge variation? Both provinces have laws prohibiting the disposal of organic materials in landfills or incinerators. While some people do the right thing voluntarily, strong public policies ensure that everybody gets on board.

### RECAP

After years of being ignored, the environmental imperative of reducing consumption may be ready to hit the mainstream. Recent opinion polls reveal that 88% of Americans believe their society is too materialistic and too focused on shopping. Almost nine out of ten Americans recognize that this excessive materialism consumes too many resources, produces too much waste, and harms the environment. Zero waste is a powerful antidote to this affluenza. By striving towards the goal of zero waste, you can help conserve natural resources, save energy, protect wild species, reduce air and water pollution, and slow down the juggernaut of climate change.

Every person's efforts can make a surprisingly substantial difference. The total impact of your efforts to reduce consumption can be multiplied to reflect the vast amount of energy and resource use being avoided at the global level. According to our estimates, if you reduce your household waste from 400 kilograms (880 pounds) to 40 kilograms (88 pounds) per year (a 90% reduction), you not only save 360 kilograms (792 pounds) from being dumped or incinerated, you create a product (compost) that enriches the Earth and a stream of raw materials (recyclables) that feeds the economy. Even more impressively, you are indirectly saving about 72,000 kilograms (158,400 pounds) of energy and resources from being chewed up by the industrial economy and spat out as pollution and waste. That's roughly the weight of a fully loaded transport truck that you could save every year. Your home will likely be less cluttered and you'll get a welcome psychological boost from doing the right thing. We encourage you to take the zero waste challenge and see how close you can get.

At the same time, we recognize that in today's circumstances only the most dedicated individuals can achieve close to zero waste. Too many products are poorly designed, there is too much wasteful packaging, and recycling/composting programs are simply not up to the challenge. It will be difficult to achieve zero waste until:

- Manufacturers redesign their products and packaging and assume responsibility for taking them back at the end of their useful life.
- Governments pass laws mandating recycled content in products.
- Subsidies for virgin materials are eliminated.
- Recycling and composting programs are improved.

The need for these policy changes reinforces the fact that while individual action to reduce ecological footprints is important, we must also seek progress at the political level. In Canada, the U.S., and Europe, some leading communities have already reduced the amount of waste going to dumps or being incinerated by half or two-thirds. How did they do it? Are citizens of these communities more ecologically aware? No, not necessarily. But there are laws, policies, plans, and programs in these places that push the envelope, prohibiting certain actions, and providing incentives for environmentally friendly behavior and technology.

Do laws really matter? Consider laws that require a refundable deposit on some beverage containers. In American states without laws requiring a deposit, the recycling rate is 27.9%. In the ten states where the deposit is five cents, the recycling rate is 70%. In Michigan, where the deposit is ten cents, the recycling rate is 95%. So yes, laws do matter, and as the next chapter will show, you can use your power as a citizen to make the world a cleaner, greener, more sustainable place.

# 6

# Citizen Green

*The strongest force on earth is not an army*
*or a police force or a government or a corporation—*
*it is ourselves, awakened to the dangers we face*
*and the possibilities we are creating. We are everywhere.*

ALEX STEFFEN

❧ ❧ ❧

In addition to your role as an ecologically informed consumer, you have
an important role to play as a citizen. Urgent political action—at
all levels of government—is necessary to achieve a sustainable future.
Innovative pro-environment policies should make it easier for people and
businesses to do the right thing and harder, if not impossible, to do the
wrong thing. Governments will only implement strong environmental
policies if pushed, pulled, and prodded by the public. That means you.

Two Nobel Peace Prize winners offer powerful inspiration to individuals seeking to act on their environmental values. Wangari Maathai,
the first environmental advocate and the first African woman to win
the Nobel Peace Prize, epitomizes everything about being a green citizen. In the late 1970s, Maathai resigned from the University of Nairobi,
where she was the first female professor, to found the Greenbelt movement. By planting more than 30 million trees, the Greenbelt movement
is reforesting Africa and tackling poverty. Despite being assaulted and

imprisoned, Maathai persevered in her grassroots efforts, entered the political arena, and was elected to the Kenyan parliament in 2002. In her Nobel acceptance speech, Maathai said "Although this prize comes to me, it acknowledges the work of countless individuals and groups across the globe. They work quietly and often without recognition to protect the environment, promote democracy, defend human rights, and ensure equality between women and men. By so doing, they plant seeds of peace."

Nobel Peace Prize winner Nelson Mandela is a passionate defender of people's right to live in a healthy environment. Thanks to Mandela's leadership, South Africa was the first nation in the world to enshrine the human right to clean water in its constitution. At that time, in the mid-1990s, 14 million people in South Africa lacked access to clean water. Today, clean water flows in the homes of more than 10 million of those people and it's expected that the gap will be closed entirely within a few years. Speaking at the World Summit on Sustainable Development in 2002, Mandela said, "When I return, as I often do, to the rural village and area of my childhood and youth, the poverty of the people and the devastation of the natural environment painfully strike me. And in that impoverishment of the natural environment, it is the absence of access to clean water that strikes most starkly. That our government has made significant progress in bringing potable water nearer to so many more people than was previously the case, I rate amongst the most important achievements of democracy in our country."

### WHAT YOU CAN DO

In contrast to Wangari Maathai and Nelson Mandela, Canadians, Americans, Australians, Europeans, and many others in the industrialized world are fortunate to live in societies where rights such as free speech and freedom of assembly are respected and protected. With a handful of troubling exceptions, we are able to actively and publicly criticize governments and businesses without fear of negative consequences.

There are nine ways you can take advantage of these freedoms and exercise your powers as a citizen on behalf of the environment:

1. Voting in elections for all levels of government.
2. Speaking up among friends and colleagues, in public, and through the media.
3. Volunteering in support of environmental causes.
4. Donating time, money, or assets to nonprofit organizations.
5. Pursuing a green career in business, government, or with an environmental group.
6. Investing ethically.
7. Participating in community events.
8. Boycotting specific products or companies.
9. Advocating for laws and policies that could help save the planet.

## VOTE FOR PEOPLE WHO ARE ECOLOGICALLY LITERATE

Although public concern about environmental issues is hitting new heights, we keep electing politicians who are ecologically illiterate and lack passion for nature. You can help reverse this situation by learning where candidates stand on environmental issues in local, state, provincial, and national elections. Then exercise your right to vote! Governments play an essential role in our lives and are critical to achieving a sustainable future. Voting is a simple act that can have huge positive or negative environmental consequences. Anyone skeptical about the impact of electoral politics should reflect on the American presidential election of 2000, where spoiled ballots, low voter turnout, and votes for Ralph Nader contributed to the election of the most anti-environmental president in American history, George W. Bush. (Of course, one might argue that by losing to Mr. Bush, Al Gore was transformed into a climate change crusader, earning a Nobel Prize. But had Gore been president, the U.S. stance on climate would have been radically different).

At the same time that the global environmental crisis is worsening, the U.K., Canada, and the U.S. are experiencing a steady erosion of the proportion of the public that votes, a pattern that is bad at the national level, worse at the state and provincial level, and downright atrocious at the local level. Voter turnout in the U.K. has been declining steadily since 1950. In Canada's 2004 federal election, voter turnout dropped to 61%, the lowest level since 1898. Canada ranked seventy-seventh in the world in voter turnout between 1945 and 2000, while the U.S. ranked one hundred and thirty-ninth. In municipal elections, only 40% of citizens vote in Canada and turnout is often even lower in the U.S. Young people express the deepest environmental concerns, yet are the least likely to vote.

By contrast, Australia has one of the highest voter turnouts in the world, in part because voting has been compulsory since the 1920s. Western Europe also has generally good voter turnout.

Clearly, electoral reforms are needed in Canada, the U.K., and the U.S. to revitalize democracy and allow citizens' voices to be heard. All three nations employ a variation on the antiquated "first past the post" electoral system. Only a small number of western democracies continue to rely on this system, which wastes many votes and often fails to reflect the intentions of a majority of voters. For example, in Canada, majority governments have been elected both federally and provincially with less than 40% of the popular vote. In other words, almost two out of three people vote against a party, yet that party gains complete control of government. Small parties with a strong national presence can garner large numbers of votes yet still be completely shut out of government, as is the case with Canada's Green Party.

Electoral systems based on proportional representation are now predominant globally. In proportional representation, parties earn seats based on their share of the popular vote, dramatically reducing the number of wasted votes. Proportional representation helped the Green Party become a powerful political force in Europe. The Green Party has been part of national coalition governments in Germany, Finland, Belgium, France, Ireland, and the Netherlands. Several Canadian provinces—including British Columbia, Quebec, Ontario, Prince Edward Island, and New Brunswick—are actively considering adopting proportional representation. Add your voice to the chorus calling for a more representative democratic system. Visit Fair Vote Canada (www. fairvotecanada.org), the U.S. site for FairVote (The Center for Voting and Democracy, www.fairvote.org), or the U.K. site for Make Votes Count (www.makemyvotecount.org.uk).

Several organizations focus their activities on promoting victory for pro-environment candidates and defeat for anti-environment candidates, regardless of their party affiliation. In the U.S., the League of Conservation Voters (LCV) tracks the voting records of Members of Congress on environmental issues and publishes an annual report card. This provides a useful guide to help decide who will get your vote. LCV has helped defeat twenty-three out of thirty-seven candidates identified as rabidly anti-environmental in the past decade, while over 80% of the candidates endorsed by LCV were elected. Conservation Voters, based on the same concept, is a Canadian organization that endorses pro-environment candidates at the municipal, provincial, and federal levels. Most of the candidates endorsed by Conservation Voters, supported by leaflets, publicity, and door-knocking campaigns, are victorious. See www.lcv.org and www. conservationvoters.ca.

### Inspiration

In a campaign led by the World Wildlife Fund and the Canadian Parks and Wilderness Society, more than a million Canadians signed a document called the Wilderness Charter in the early 1990s, urging governments to protect at least 12% of the country in parks by 2000. All political leaders and governments pledged to achieve the goal. The public pressure contributed to tremendous growth in Canadian parks and protected areas, which are now safe from industrial resource extraction. During the 1990s, more than one thousand new parks, ecological reserves, and wilderness areas were established, covering more than 40 million hectares (almost 100 million acres).

In Australia, pressure by environmental groups and concerned citizens led to legislation protecting more than 20 million hectares of native bushland from being cleared.

## SPEAK UP

There have never been so many opportunities to voice your opinion. You can communicate directly with elected representatives and civil servants by phone, fax, mail, or email. You can share your views publicly by:

- Writing letters to the editors of newspapers and magazines.
- Calling radio programs.
- Posting messages or videos on the Internet.
- Writing your own blog.
- Creating your own website.

When enough people speak up, governments usually listen. Recent examples include the defeat of proposals that would have weakened standards for organic food in the U.S. (more than five hundred thousand people spoke up in opposition), the defeat of a shadowy deal called the Multilateral Agreement on Investment because of worldwide protests, and the demise of Canada's Orwellian Clean Air Act when the public and the media realized that the proposed legislation was in fact a recipe for dirty air.

One of the challenges facing environmental advocates is that public support is wide but shallow. When it comes to stronger laws for clean air, clean water, and endangered species, most members of the public are on board. However, it's a silent majority. In contrast, the vocal minority that opposes stronger environmental protection usually has money at stake and is highly motivated to speak out. This is why London, Washington, Ottawa, Canberra, and state and provincial capitals around the world are crawling with highly paid corporate lobbyists who regularly meet with politicians and civil servants to block proposed pro-environmental policies.

If every citizen who supports a stable climate, clean air, clean water, and a healthy environment took the time to send just one hand-written letter (an endangered species in its own right) to their political leaders every year it would make an enormous difference. That's a time commitment of less than five seconds a day, so no matter how busy you are, it's doable. As an added incentive for Canadians, no stamp is required on letters addressed to Members of Parliament.

Governments discriminate between different kinds of correspondence. Postcards, form letters, and generic email messages have the least impact. Hand-written letters, telephone calls, and face-to-face conversations have the greatest impact. Your communication has a much larger impact than you would imagine. Bureaucrats and politicians know that for every letter or phone call they receive, dozens or hundreds of others share the same view but haven't taken the time to write or call.

An important point to remember is that the politicians and civil servants are human beings. Politeness and an occasional pat on the back will go a long way. Think about how you can help these officials help the environment by offering anything from a friendly letter to the editor to some policy advice from a respected source. Recognize that politicians and civil servants may actually share your environmental values. European surveys show that both citizens and political decision-makers overwhelmingly prefer environmentally friendly transport. But when asked about the other group's preferences, only 41% thought that the other group favored environmentally friendly transport.

When writing to politicians, civil servants, and elected representatives, consider the following letter-writing tips:
· Be passionate but polite.
· Be brief (no more than two pages).
· Write to the appropriate person.
· Make a clear and specific request.
· Ask for a response.

Speaking up is not limited to communicating with government. You can tell businesses why you refuse to purchase their products and urge them to make pro-environment changes. You can talk with your friends, relatives, teammates, neighbors, fellow churchgoers, and co-workers about what you've learned on environmental issues. Imagine the impact if every person committed to educating two people about a particular environmental issue, each of those persons made a similar commitment, and so on. Starting on the first day of the month, two new people would be engaged. On the second day, four new people would be brought on board. By the end of the month, in just thirty days, over 1 billion people could be reached.

### VOLUNTEER

Volunteers in Canada provide over 2 billion hours of their time to various causes annually, equal to about 1 million full-time jobs. However, less than 1% of Canadians who volunteer do so for an environmental organization. The situation is similar in the U.S., while in Australia, one in forty volunteer hours are dedicated to environmental causes. In the U.K., between 4% and 8% of volunteers are engaged in protecting the environment.

Volunteering with an environmental group can be an incredibly rewarding experience. Most environmental organizations have no paid staff and depend on the generosity of people who volunteer, so there are opportunities galore. Try attending the meetings of several different organizations to see if you like the people and to get a feel for where your skills might best be applied. Local organizations often offer opportunities for hands-on experiences, from restoring salmon streams to working on a newsletter. You might get to do a job that will look good on your resume. You might get to spend time outdoors and meet interesting people. Of course, whatever volunteer path you choose, your level of involvement will depend on your personal circumstances. Maybe you're a student or a senior with time to help out on a regular basis. Perhaps your time is tight and you can only assist with annual events like beach cleanups. Either way, you will be making a contribution.

# CONTACT GOVERNMENT OFFICIALS

### PRIME MINISTER OF AUSTRALIA
PO Box 6022
House of Representatives
Canberra, ACT 2600
Email: www.pm.gov.au/contact/index.cfm
Phone: 02-6277-7700 · Fax: 02-6273-4100
To contact other Australian elected representatives,
visit www.aph.gov.au/library/tutorial/contact.htm.

### PRIME MINISTER OF CANADA
80 Wellington Street
Ottawa, ON K1A 0A2
Email: pm@pm.gc.ca
Phone: 613-992-4211 · Fax: 613-941-6900
To contact other Canadian elected representatives, visit http://canada.gc.ca/
directories/direct_e.html#mp or Democracy Watch www.dwatch.ca.

### PRIME MINISTER OF THE UNITED KINGDOM
10 Downing Street
London SW1 2AA
Email: www.nuntber=10.gov.uk/output/page821.asp
Fax: 020-7925-0918
To contact other elected representatives in the U.K.,
visit www.parliament.uk/about/contacting/mp.cfm.

### PRESIDENT OF THE UNITED STATES
1600 Pennsylvania Avenue NW
Washington, DC 20500
Email: president@whitehouse.gov or comments@whitehouse.gov

Phone: 202-456-1111 or 202-456-1414 · Fax: 202-456-2461
To contact other elected representatives in the U.S., visit www.senate.gov,
www.house.gov, or www.vote-smart.org.

### SAMPLE LETTER ON CLIMATE CHANGE

Dear President/Prime Minister

I am a citizen with serious concerns about your lack of effective action to address climate change. Scientific reports make it clear that climate change is the most serious environmental problem facing our planet. Our country has one of the worst records in the world in terms of per capita contributions to the problem, with much higher emissions than citizens in other nations. We cannot continue to use the Earth's atmosphere as a dumping ground for emissions of carbon dioxide and other greenhouse gases.

I would like you to do everything in your power to take the following actions:

1. Impose a carbon tax on all fossil fuels and use the revenue generated to ensure the rapid development and adoption of renewable energy.
2. Place strict limits on carbon dioxide emissions from industry.
3. Enact the world's strongest standards for the energy efficiency of vehicles, buildings, and all consumer products that use energy.

These policies have been successful, environmentally and economically, in other western industrialized nations, including Norway, Japan, and Germany.

I would appreciate a written reply outlining your response to these proposals.

Respectfully,
Name
Address

The Internet is a great source of environmental volunteer opportunities in your own country and in other parts of the world. You can see some examples at www.idealist.org, www.volunteer.ca, www.conservation volunteers.com.au, and www.do-it.org.uk.

Another option is to volunteer with a local or national political organization. It's surprisingly easy to participate in the electoral process by doing one of the following:

- Join a political party. Put forward motions at the local or national level in favor of strong environmental policies and practices.
- Volunteer to support a candidate who offers a strong environmental platform.
- Help a nongovernmental organization attempt to influence the environmental platform of a particular candidate or party.

### Inspiration

A grassroots movement to reduce the health and environmental threats posed by the unnecessary use of pesticides recently caught fire in Canada. Spurred into action by the passionate advocacy of local residents, predominantly volunteers, more than 125 Canadian municipalities and the entire province of Quebec passed laws restricting the use of pesticides. Chemical companies challenged the laws in court but the Supreme Court of Canada upheld their validity, stating "our common future, that of every Canadian community, depends on a healthy environment," which all levels of government have a responsibility to protect. The campaign won't end until every Canadian is protected by regulations that put children's health ahead of dandelion-free lawns.

### DONATE

With the exception of a few well-funded organizations, most environmental groups struggle to stay afloat from year to year. Although 85% of Canadians give money to charitable organizations, only 2% of the funds go to environmental groups. American statistics are similar. In the U.K. and Australia, 3% to 5% of donations from individuals go to protecting

the environment, while less than 1% of donations from businesses go
to the environment. Despite chronic underfunding, environmentalists
win many important victories by relentlessly campaigning for cleaner air,
cleaner water, more responsible resource management, and the protection of nature's amazing diversity. Donations from concerned citizens
are the financial lifeblood of most groups. If you would like to donate to
an environmental cause, consider the following:

· Focus on a few organizations that you respect.
· Become a monthly donor, providing a stable source of income that
  assists groups in financial and strategic planning. Even ten dollars a
  month will be appreciated.
· Donate stocks, bonds, and land and receive considerable tax benefits.
· Leave an environmental legacy in your will.

### Inspiration

A wild and beautiful region of coastal British Columbia, formerly
known as the Mid-coast Timber Supply Area, was renamed the Great
Bear Rainforest in the mid-1990s by savvy environmentalists. After a
decade of concerted effort supported by the local First Nations, including boycotts, letter-writing campaigns, protests, and lobbying, a land-
mark agreement was signed in 2007. The agreement designates more
than one hundred protected areas covering roughly 5 million acres and
places strict controls on resource extraction in another 19 million acres.
A unique element of the deal was that environmentalists and government each chipped in $60 million to finance conservation management
and ecologically sustainable business ventures in the region. Dozens of
rainforest valleys full of wild salmon, wolves, grizzly bears, black bears,
and the rare white spirit bear are now protected from the threat of logging, mining, and other industrial activities.

### PARTICIPATE IN COMMUNITY ACTIVITIES

The sky's the limit when it comes to creative community events that can
contribute to raising environmental awareness, reducing the size of our

collective ecological footprint, or putting pressure on governments and businesses to go green. A few examples include:

- Weekend block parties that close your street to motorized traffic.
- Fundraising events such as bake sales, raffles, runs or walks, bottle drives, collective garage sales, or cell phone recycling projects.
- Guest speaker events at a local library, college, or community hall.
- Forums on clean transportation or greening your neighborhood.
- Local litter cleanup, or ecological restoration projects.
- A community gardening event.
- An Earth Day parade.
- Events connected to Clean Air Day, Rivers Day, Oceans Day, Buy Nothing Day, Car-free Day, and TV Turnoff Week.

If you have the time and inclination, you can go beyond participating by helping to organize some of these events. In addition to enjoying community activities for their own sake, you'll meet interesting people and learn things you never dreamed of knowing.

### BOYCOTT A PRODUCT OR A COMPANY

We vote for businesses by spending money rather than marking ballots. A boycott attempts to achieve certain objectives by persuading individuals not to support a business or a nation. Boycotts can be powerful tools for raising awareness about the impact of environmentally destructive practices or policies, human rights abuses, and unfair labor practices. The bus boycott organized by Dr. Martin Luther King in Montgomery, Alabama, was a defining moment in the civil rights era. Public attitudes, business practices, and political history were changed by the United Farm Workers boycott of table grapes (begun by Cesar Chavez in the 1960s), the boycott of Nestle over inappropriate marketing of infant formula in less economically developed countries, and the boycott of South Africa because of apartheid. Corporate executives admit that boycotts are the most effective weapons wielded by consumers.

An example of a boycott currently enjoying a high profile is the campaign against ExxonMobil, the multinational oil giant. The ExxonMobil boycott, led by eighteen environmental organizations, including Greenpeace, the Sierra Club, and the Natural Resources Defense Council, calls on the company to stop opposing mandatory reductions in greenhouse gas emissions and stop funding junk science that denies the reality of climate change. If you are interested in organizing a boycott, download Co-op America's excellent Boycott Organizer's Guide, available free from www.boycotts.org.

### CHOOSE A GREEN CAREER

There have never been so many opportunities to work in the environmental field. In Canada, more than half a million people are employed in green jobs, and over one hundred thousand organizations have at least one environmental employee. The green industry in the U.S. in 2005 employed 1.6 million people and was worth $265 billion. The wind and solar energy industries are growing by 20% to 30% a year globally and have created more than one hundred and thirty thousand jobs in Germany alone during the past decade.

The scope and scale of environmental challenges mean that whatever skill set you possess, there is environmental work available. Conventional options include working for environmental organizations, green businesses, governments, and international institutions. Emerging professions include emissions brokers, biomimicry chemists and engineers (seeking to emulate natural wonders such as photosynthesis or spiders' silk), sustainability coordinators, and green architects. If you're interested in law, there are firms specializing in environmental law, environmental departments in large law firms, and opportunities to hang out your own shingle and do environmental work. If you're a gardener, municipalities striving to keep their cities beautiful without pesticides need you. If you possess entrepreneurial zeal, figure out a way to create social value at the same time that you make money. There are environmental employment opportunities for teachers, doctors, scientists, policy experts, farmers, architects, builders, nutritionists, travel agents, politicians, and sales-people. The list is endless. The first steps are finding out about these opportunities and talking to somebody already doing the kind of work you would like to do.

## INVEST ETHICALLY

Although many environmentally concerned individuals throughout the world invest in stocks, bonds, and real estate, few of these investments are consistent with environmental values. In many cases, investors are providing financial support for corporations that wreak havoc on the planet. Fortunately, there is rapid growth in the field of socially respon-sible investing, from ethical mutual funds to programs run by progressive financial institutions. Socially responsible investing considers environ-mental sustainability, labor practices, human rights, and corporate gov-ernance along with traditional investment analysis. In Canada, assets invested according to socially responsible guidelines are growing rapidly, from $65 billion in 2004 to $504 billion in 2006. In the U.S., socially responsible investments soared from $639 billion in 1995 to $2.29 trillion in 2005, making up one in ten dollars under professional financial man-agement. Ethical investments are also booming in Australia and the U.K.

Socially responsible investing includes three main elements:
1. Screening. This involves evaluating potential investments on the basis of social and environmental criteria (e.g., respect for human rights, compliance with environmental laws, safe and useful products or ser-vices).
2. Shareholder advocacy. Advocacy strategies include resolutions, proxy voting, and other means to influence corporate policies or actions. This approach succeeded in pressuring many corporations to pull out of South Africa in protest against apartheid.
3. Community investing. This directs capital to communities underserved by traditional financial services, providing access to credit, equity, capital, and basic banking products that these communities lack. The

Nobel Prize–winning microcredit programs of Muhammad Yunus and the Grameen Bank are a superb example of community investing.

Socially responsible investing enables you to align financial goals and personal values. Happily, investing in socially and environmentally responsible corporations can provide a higher return on investment. A comprehensive review of more than fifty studies concluded that there is a "universally positive" relationship between corporate social/environmental performance and corporate financial performance. The Domini 400 Social Index (U.S.) and the Jantzi Social Index (Canada) have both outperformed mainstream stock indices since their inception (1990 and 2000, respectively). Websites such as www.socialfunds.com offer excellent resources on socially responsible investing. In Australia and New Zealand, see www.responsibleinvestment.org. In Canada, see www.socialinvestment.ca. In the U.K., see www.uksif.org. In the U.S., see www.socialinvest.org. Another simple step is to choose a socially and environmentally friendly bank or credit union.

### ADVOCATE FOR POLICIES THAT COULD SAVE THE PLANET

Although voluntary changes in individual behavior are important, laws and policies are needed to encourage or compel everybody to adopt sustainable actions. Pressure from individuals, ranging in number from a small handful to millions of people, has prompted encouraging environmental policy changes at the local, regional, national, and international levels. Ten policies have already been successful in some part of the world and need to be emulated everywhere:

1. Create a bold vision of a sustainable future.
2. Replace fossil fuels with renewable energy.
3. Move towards a waste-free economy.
4. Mandate safe substitutes for health-harming chemicals.
5. Set high environmental standards and raise the bar regularly.
6. Make the market work by using taxes and subsidies to discourage environmentally damaging activities and promote healthy alternatives.

7. Plan vibrant, green communities.
8. Promote a healthy diet.
9. Make ecological literacy a cornerstone of our education system.
10. Measure society's progress according to things that really matter, not just gross domestic product.

### 1. Create a Bold Vision of a Sustainable Future

One of the most inspiring actions a community can take is to create a compelling long-term vision of what a sustainable future looks like and a detailed plan for getting there. In 1998, Sweden passed a law setting out broad environmental objectives that it seeks to achieve within the time frame of one generation (twenty-five years). These objectives—such as clean air, good quality groundwater, a nontoxic environment, a rich diversity of plant and animal life, and a magnificent mountain landscape—enjoy universal support. Specific targets were set for the short and medium term to make sure Sweden stays on track or identifies areas where stronger effort is required. Every year, an expert committee reviews Sweden's progress.

Sweden is clearly a world leader in moving towards a sustainable future. By 2006, Sweden reduced greenhouse gas emissions to 7.2% below 1990 levels, going beyond its commitment under the Kyoto Protocol. Sweden has dramatically reduced emissions of sulfur dioxide (the main cause of acid rain), the use of highly toxic pesticides, and the amount of garbage going to landfills. At the same time, the World Economic Forum ranks Sweden ahead of the U.S., Canada, Australia, and the U.K. in economic competitiveness.

### 2. Replace Fossil Fuels with Renewable Energy

Compared with today's destructive dependence on fossil fuels, the use of renewable energy offers:
- Minimal climate, environmental, and health effects instead of massive negative impacts.

- A permanent supply of energy instead of a diminishing supply.
- Widely distributed resources instead of oil, gas, and coal reserves concentrated in a few nations.
- Prices that are falling consistently over time (thanks to mass production and technological improvement) instead of rising unpredictably.

Germany and Japan are world leaders in renewable energy because of innovative policies. Germany's feed-in tariff is a law requiring energy suppliers to buy electricity from renewable sources at a premium price for a fixed period of time. This law guarantees investment security, supports all viable renewable energy technologies, and is widely regarded as the best policy for spurring the growth of renewable energy. Germany is among the top three nations in the world in both wind and solar energy generation, and will meet its targets under the Kyoto Protocol. According to Stefan Dietrich, spokesperson for a German solar manufacturer, "the feed-in tariff changed everything—it is that simple." Feed-in tariffs have spread to most of the European Union and more than forty countries worldwide.

In the 1990s, Japan and Germany launched massive solar roof initiatives, using consumer subsidies to make solar electricity competitive with conventional sources. As the costs of solar photovoltaic systems fell, the Japanese government gradually reduced the amount of the subsidy. By 2005, solar energy was competitive with other sources of electricity in Japan and the subsidies were discontinued. Both Japan and Germany are world leaders in solar power and have hundreds of thousands of rooftop solar installations. California Governor Arnold Schwarzenegger signed a Million Solar Roofs bill in 2006, committing over $3 billion to achieving the goal by 2018.

### 3. Move Towards a Waste-free Economy

Two recent European laws incorporate a revolutionary and successful approach to eliminating waste. The first law enacts a concept called extended producer responsibility, making manufacturers responsible for taking back their products (e.g., motor vehicles, electronic equipment, and computers) when consumers no longer want them. This law puts the onus on manufacturers to redesign their products and processes in ways that completely eliminate waste and pollution. For example, by 2015, 95% of the materials in cars, by weight, must be recyclable or reusable.

The second law requires the elimination of hazardous substances—including mercury, lead, cadmium, and toxic flame retardants—from consumer products. In essence, these two laws implement the revolutionary cradle-to-cradle approach discussed in Chapter 1, wherein everything we make must be reusable, recyclable, or safely biodegradable. Because Europe is such a large market for so many products, these laws are having a global impact.

### 4. Mandate Safe Substitutes for Health-harming Chemicals

Industrial chemicals and the by-products of burning fossil fuels are linked to many chronic diseases, including cancer, neurological disorders (e.g., Parkinson's disease, Alzheimer's disease), cardiovascular disease, respiratory illness, and reproductive problems. The compelling evidence of adverse health effects led Sweden to pioneer the substitution principle, which requires corporations to replace hazardous chemicals with safer substances whenever alternatives are available. The substitution principle is now the law throughout Europe.

Europe has already required the substitution of safer alternatives for hundreds of hazardous substances still used in Australia, the U.S., Canada, and other parts of the world, including:

· Pesticides (e.g., atrazine, 1,3-dichloropropene, permethrin).
· Asbestos, a deadly cancer-causing substance.
· Phthalates used in cosmetic products, toys, and other children's products.
· Nonylphenols in cleaning products.
· Brominated flame retardants (PBDEs) that disrupt the hormone system.

Fashion and cosmetics retailer H&M, with more than thirteen hundred stores in twenty-eight countries, is a vocal proponent of the substitution principle. H&M voluntarily eliminated the sale of products containing the following dangerous synthetic chemicals and heavy metals: brominated flame retardants; alkyl phenyl ethoxylates; polyvinyl chloride (PVC); organotins; azo dyes; bisphenol A; phthalates; antimony, mercury, and lead; and many chlorinated aromatic hydrocarbons. A spokesperson for the company said, "We have found that almost anything is possible as long as you set clear guidelines on what is not acceptable."

### 5. Set High Environmental Standards and Raise the Bar Regularly

Setting and enforcing high standards is a powerful way to achieve environmental progress. The wealthy nations of the world need to adopt zero energy building codes, zero emission standards for vehicles, and super-efficiency rules for products of all kinds, from light bulbs to refrigerators. The U.K. is considering amendments to the national building code that would require all new construction to produce zero carbon dioxide emissions from energy use by 2016. Japan is renowned for its Top Runner law, which identifies the most energy-efficient products and makes all manufacturers meet the higher standard set by those products within a certain period of time. This law helped make Japanese efficiency standards among the highest in the world for products ranging from vehicles to refrigerators. According to the International Energy Agency, electricity use in Canada and the U.S. could be reduced 24% in seven years through stronger energy efficiency policies. The reduction in electricity use would prevent the emission of 322 million metric tons of carbon dioxide, equivalent to taking 100 million cars off the roads, and would have a "negative cost" to consumers, meaning you'd save money.

The flip side of high standards for energy efficiency is that the least efficient and most polluting products should be banned. Some governments are already moving to restrict or prohibit the sale of products with unnecessarily large ecological footprints, such as incandescent light bulbs, plastic bags, and low-efficiency furnaces. Some cities prohibit noisy and noxious gas-powered items such as leaf blowers, lawn mowers, and jet skis.

## 6. Make the Market Work

Corporations, individuals, and governments that pollute or waste resources don't pay for the ecological harm they cause. Two key policies for making polluters and nature despoilers pay are shifting taxes and subsidies to discourage harmful actions and promoting sustainable alternatives. By cutting taxes on employment and investment and taxing pollution and waste, governments can restructure the economy in a way that makes sense both ecologically and economically. European nations lead the world in shifting taxes onto pollution, pesticides, and toxic chemicals. Because of the urgency of the climate crisis, carbon taxes are critical. Carbon taxes send a powerful signal to use energy more efficiently and switch to clean energy. For example, carbon taxes raise the price of gasoline and diesel, providing a clear incentive to purchase fuel-efficient vehicles and switch from driving to transit, cycling, or other green options. Carbon taxes are already used in many European nations, including Norway, Sweden, Finland, France, and Italy.

A tremendous amount of ecological damage could be avoided if governments stopped making it artificially cheap to carry out destructive activities. Annual subsidies to the energy industry amount to many billions of dollars. For every dollar dedicated to fossil fuels, only pennies are provided for renewable energy subsidies. Ocean experts believe that if governments pulled the plug on subsidies for deep-sea trawling, the damaging practice would no longer be economically viable. There are harmful subsidies to individuals as well as corporations. For example, in the U.S., vehicles that generally have the worst fuel efficiency—SUVs, trucks, and minivans—are exempt from the $7,000 federal gas guzzler tax. Globally, the hundreds of billions of dollars in subsidies allocated to environmentally damaging activities should be redirected to renewable energy, zero carbon buildings, zero emission vehicles, cradle-to-cradle products, and local, organic foods.

### 7. Plan Vibrant, Green Communities

Urban sprawl causes a witches' brew of environmental, social, and economic problems. The antidote to sprawl is smart growth, a bundle of land use and development principles that enhance quality of life, protect the environment, and save money by reducing energy and infrastructure costs. Smart growth focuses on increasing density, ensuring mixed development that integrates businesses and residences, making priorities of public transit, cycling, and walking, and protecting green space, natural beauty, and farmland. Applying smart growth principles results in neighborhoods that are safe, attractive, affordable, convenient, and healthy. Making public transit more attractive is essential and can be achieved by:
· Improving service and reliability.
· Giving buses priority on roads.
· Lowering or even eliminating fares.
· Imposing or raising congestion taxes, road tolls, vehicle sales taxes, and fuel taxes.
· Eliminating hidden subsidies for private vehicles (e.g., free parking).

Smart growth works. Dense, convenient areas like North Beach in San Francisco reduce vehicle kilometers traveled by 75% when compared with suburban communities. Applying smart growth principles to all new housing in the U.S. for the next decade would provide an eye-popping $2 trillion in cost savings compared with the cost of conventional development. The savings are due to lower levels of car ownership, fewer vehicle kilometers traveled, and reduced energy costs.

### 8. Promote a Healthy Diet

To date, efforts to promote healthy eating have been anemic, overwhelmed by super-sized corporate promotion of unhealthy food. Some jurisdictions are starting to turn the tide by banning junk food in schools, eliminating particularly harmful ingredients such as trans fats, and pro-hibiting advertising aimed at young children. There is still a long way to go. A comprehensive package of policies is needed to move from today's unhealthy and environmentally destructive diets towards nutritious and sustainable food choices.

For starters, governments should reallocate subsidies currently expended on conventional crops, livestock, and genetically modified organisms (GMOs) to organic agriculture and local food. Taxes on junk foods would generate revenue to promote healthy food. It would also help to make food labels meaningful by requiring accurate information about serving sizes, the country of origin, adverse health effects, the presence of GMOs, and carbon footprints. Canada, the U.S., and other industrialized countries should adopt European bans on using antibiot-ics to promote faster animal growth and feeding arsenic to chickens.

Another key element in promoting a healthy diet is starting young, ensuring that children eat nutritious and sustainable food. School lunch programs should offer high-quality food with maximum local and organic content and limited quantities of meat. The American Acad-emy of Pediatrics believes that "advertising directed at children is inher-ently deceptive and exploits children under eight years of age." Sweden prohibited all television advertising aimed at children under the age of twelve in 1991. In 2007, the U.K. banned television ads for food and drinks high in fat, sugar, or salt during programs aimed at children aged four to nine, while a broader ban comes into force in 2008. Advertising unhealthy food products to children should be universally prohibited.

### 9. Make Ecological Literacy a Cornerstone of Education

The majority of citizens in many industrialized countries are unin-formed or misinformed about environmental topics. More than one in seven Americans believe the oceans are a source of fresh water and only 12% can pass a basic quiz on energy topics. In Australia, studies show that most primary school teachers are ecologically illiterate, with no training in environmental education. Nations with the highest level of ecological literacy tend to have the best environmental records, while nations with poor levels of ecological literacy have worse records. In recent years, the already minimal budgets for environmental education in many parts of the U.S. and Canada have been reduced. Ontario is one bright light with its integration of environmental education into all courses in all grades, following the comprehensive recommendations of an expert group led by Canadian astronaut Roberta Bondar. And Australia has published an inspiring strategy document, *Education for a Sustainable Future*, which outlines a comprehensive national environmental education program for Australia schools.

Today's children are tomorrow's citizens and will inherit a world with complex environmental challenges ranging from the local to the global. It is imperative that every child be able not only to read and write but also to understand where their drinking water comes from, where their garbage goes, and how processes such as climate change work. Environmentally knowledgeable people are far more likely to recycle, avoid pesticides, and save energy in the home. Improving the environmental awareness of a majority of Americans would produce an estimated $75 billion per year in reduced expenses on energy, water, and health care. As added incentive, studies indicate that children enrolled in environmental education programs achieve higher performance in reading, writing, math, and science. Environmental education should be a mandatory part of the curriculum from kindergarten through grade 12.

### 10. Measure Society's Progress
### According to Things That Really Matter

A recent article in the *The Economist* says that gross domestic product (GDP), the most commonly used measure of a country's success, "is badly flawed as a guide to a nation's economic well-being." GDP overlooks many of the things that people value most, including trust, respect, community, clean air, clean water, beauty, and compassion. Worse yet,

GDP treats crime, cancer, environmental destruction, and war as positive because of expenditures on criminal justice and policing, health care, cleaning up oils spills and hazardous waste sites, and the military.

Canada, the U.K., and Australia are experimenting with more holistic measures, such as the genuine progress index, in an attempt to meaningfully assess the social, economic, and environmental state of affairs. The genuine progress index incorporates data on health, leisure, volunteer activities, income distribution, air and water quality, and dozens of other indicators. Japan and Switzerland are incorporating the ecological footprint concept into their national accounting systems to monitor progress towards a sustainable future. In the Buddhist kingdom of Bhutan, the primary national goal is to achieve greater happiness for the people, as measured by a gross national happiness index. Independent assessments of happiness find that this strategy is working. Despite per capita incomes of about $2,000, Bhutanese are happier than Americans or Canadians. By pointing society in a different direction, measuring what really matters to people could have a revolutionary impact.

## RECAP

For many of the subjects covered in this book, you may feel frustrated that your preferred choice is either unavailable or unaffordable. For example, the only energy choice offered by your utility may be electricity from a coal-fired plant, or the premium for green power may be prohibitively expensive. This is an untenable situation. Green power and other environmentally friendly choices should be available to everyone at a competitive price. The only way to address the problem of unavailable and unaffordable choices is to use your power as a citizen.

The policies outlined in this chapter need a push. Ask your elected representatives to establish a process for envisioning a sustainable future. Challenge governments at all levels to spark the shift to renewable energy. Support businesses that "get it" and are striving to minimize their ecological footprints. Push governments and businesses to eliminate waste and pollution.

We live in democratic societies where your vote, your voice, and your choices can make a big difference. It might be easier to throw in the towel and watch "American Idol" or some other mind-numbing television program instead of getting actively involved in pushing for a better future. It takes effort and courage to stand up for what you believe in. Courage, according to 1991 Nobel Peace Prize winner Aung San Suu Kyi, the democratically elected but imprisoned leader of Burma (Myanmar), has three aspects:

1. The courage to learn about what is really going on and what's important.
2. The courage to feel.
3. The courage to act.

If you've read this far, you've already shown the first part of Suu Kyi's definition of courage. Keep going! Vote. Volunteer. Donate. Speak up. Reconsider your career and your investment portfolio. Recognize that your actions will make a difference. Your vote could change the outcome of an election. Your donation could help an environmental organization win a campaign. Your letter could open a politician's eyes, or cause a business to change its practices. Your opinion could influence family members, friends, and colleagues to change some of their habits. Your purchase could help a sustainable business get off the ground. Your participation could be essential to the success of an ecological restoration project in your community. The time to get started is now. Think like a gardener. Have faith in the seeds that you plant. Although they may seem tiny, seeds can grow into incredible plants providing a dazzling array of wonders from flowers to fruit. The more effort you put into gardening or green citizenship, the more rewards you will eventually harvest.

# 7

# Smaller Footprint,
# Bigger Smile

*Study nature,, love nature,*
*stay close to nature. It will never fail you.*
FRANK LLOYD WRIGHT

❧   ❧   ❧

Climate change, declining biodiversity, and toxic pollution are daunting problems, but solutions exist. We have the technology, the values,
and the capacity to achieve a sustainable future, but we must act now
to prevent today's problems from becoming tomorrow's catastrophes. The
emergence of zero energy buildings, zero emission vehicles, zero waste,
and cradle-to-cradle products is extraordinarily exciting. Zero energy
buildings and communities are being built in Canada, the U.S., and
Europe. Zero emission vehicles are being manufactured. Zero waste is
the goal of a growing number of individuals, cities, regions, nations, and
corporations. More and more products—from diapers to office chairs—
are being made according to cradle-to-cradle principles so that they are
completely recyclable, reusable, or biodegradable. Year after year, wind
and solar power set new records for growth. These remarkable developments offer an oasis of hope in a desert of depressing environmental
news. Each of us can help propel society towards a sustainable future by

talking about these tantalizing possibilities, by demanding laws and policies that accelerate their growth, and by doing the best we can to make our ecological footprints as small as possible. Each of us can help ensure that the promise of a sustainable future for our children and our grandchildren is not a mirage.

## SPEND MORE TIME OUTDOORS

One of the easiest and, paradoxically, most important, things you can do to reduce your ecological footprint is spend more time outdoors in natural settings. Connecting with nature will inspire you to become a better steward of the planet. Whether you're working in your yard, tasting food fresh from the garden, admiring tall trees or small trees, smelling flowers, listening to the songs of birds or the music of the wind, feeling the warmth of the sun or the touch of rain on your skin, or marveling at the moon, the stars, and the clouds, you will also reap physical and psychological benefits.

The deeper your connection to nature and the more time spent outdoors, the more happy you are likely to be. Contact with nature offers an amazing variety of health benefits, including significantly longer life expectancy, reduced stress and anxiety, and accelerated recovery from illness. People who maintain a close bond with nature score higher in autonomy, vitality, personal growth, self-acceptance, positive emotions, and having a sense of purpose in life. Close connections with nature also appear to be related to increased productivity and job satisfaction.

Spending time outside is particularly vital for children. Playing outside offers not only fun and exercise but helps children develop their cognitive and motor skills. School grounds with more natural features (e.g., trees, grass, and gardens) provide more opportunities for learning and are linked to positive behavioral changes in students, including less bullying.

Consider the following no-cost and low-cost tips for connecting with nature:

- Go for regular walks, runs, bike rides, or paddles in natural settings.
- Get a book on local ecology from the library and learn about native species of birds, plants, and animals. Find out what species lived in your region one thousand years ago.
- Go for a guided tour of a local ecosystem with a biologist, ecologist, or naturalist.
- Join a local parks group or environment organization and go on their outings.
- Enjoy regular picnics at a local park, a beach, or in your yard.
- Hang a birdfeeder outside your window and learn to identify a diversity of local species.
- Take lessons in a new outdoor activity such as sea kayaking or gardening.
- Go for a local day hike or raft down a nearby river on a weekend.
- Plan a vacation around visiting a local natural wonder (e.g., a national park).
- Create wildlife habitat in your yard or on your patio or balcony by providing food, water, and shelter (e.g., plant native trees or grow flowering plants that attract native wildlife such as butterflies or hummingbirds).
- Build butterfly and vegetable gardens in every schoolyard so that children learn to love creepy-crawly things as well as the warm and fuzzy elements of nature.

### Inspiration

My (DRB) two-year-old daughter Meredith reminds me every day of the importance of connecting with nature. Ever since she was a baby, Meredith has always loved being outside. Whether we walk to the beach, splash in mud puddles, or wander around watching deer, seals, eagles, or ants, our time together in the natural world is both educational and enchanting.

One evening last fall we stepped out onto our deck under a starlit sky to investigate an unusual sound. We couldn't see them, but some otters in the woods were either mating or fighting. Meredith looked up at me, smiled, and said "Papa, the stars are singing."

The main reason many people give for not doing more outdoor activities and other things they enjoy is that they're too busy. Indeed, Americans work longer hours than citizens of any other wealthy industrialized nation. In 2006, the average American worked 1,804 hours, or 370 hours more than the average German. That's ten extra weeks of work (or holidays, from the German perspective) every year. Canadians aren't far behind, working an average of 1,738 hours annually. If you're time-poor because of work or other obligations, then you're much more likely to drive than cycle or take transit, more likely to eat fast food or junk food than prepare a healthy meal, and more likely to buy inefficient or potentially toxic products (because you lack the time to do any research). When people are time-poor, they have less time to spend on the activities that create happiness, such as socializing with friends, pursuing hobbies, and engaging with their communities.

People are working harder and harder to amass more money and material wealth, yet the evidence is clear that this is a fool's quest, providing little or no additional happiness while undermining the very qualities that make life worthwhile. American happiness has declined since 1957, despite people earning more than twice as much money (in real terms). It's no coincidence that since 1957 the divorce rate has doubled, the teen suicide rate has more than doubled, and the rate of mental illness has skyrocketed. Social scientists confirm what many people already intuitively understand: happiness comes not from money but from relationships, community, trust, and having a sense of purpose in life. The activities that are most likely to create happiness—time spent with family and friends, outdoor activities, sports, music, literature, dance, theatre and all manner of artistic endeavors, creative hobbies, and lifelong education—generally have modest ecological impacts. Our final recommendation is to take back some of your time from work, television, and shopping, and reallocate it to spending time outdoors and doing other activities that you genuinely enjoy.

# ≣ SUMMARY OF PRIORITY RECOMMENDATIONS ≣

### HOME

· Choose a modest home near work, school, recreation, and public transit.
· Get a home energy audit and follow the energy-saving recommendations.
· Buy green electricity.

### FOOD

· Choose food that is produced locally and organically.
· Eat more plant-based foods and less meat, eggs, and dairy.

### TRANSPORT

· Rack up fewer road and air kilometers by relying on green alternatives (cycling, walking, public transit, car sharing, carpooling, telecommuting, and videoconferencing).
· Drive the most fuel-efficient vehicle that meets your needs.

### STUFF

· Adopt our guiding principles of sustainable consumption.
· Reduce, reuse, and recycle (in that order).

### CITIZENSHIP

· Vote for pro-environmental candidates.
· Speak out about environmental issues.
· Donate time and money to environmental organizations.

### NATURE

· Spend more time outdoors, especially if you have children.
· Take back some of your time.

*Inspiration*

My (DS) father was my great mentor and buddy. In 1994, he knew he was dying. My mother had died ten years earlier and now as he faced his death, he was not in pain, completely unafraid of the end. I moved in to care for him the last month of his life and each night, my wife and family would arrive with treats, slides, and reminiscences. My sisters arrived during the last week and we were all present at his death. In those last days, we shared many happy memories as we laughed and cried about a man who had been so important to us all. In all that time, we never once reminded him of how wonderful a car, house, or clothing had been. All we talked of was family, friends, neighbors, and the wonderful things we did together. That's what the joy and happiness in life are all about, not material things.

## INCREASE YOUR HAPPINESS
## AND REDUCE YOUR ECOLOGICAL FOOTPRINT

Why does happiness matter from an environmental perspective? The reason is that happy people are more ecologically responsible. Happy individuals tend to be more focused on personal growth, relationships, and community involvement than on money and possessions. Happy people also tend to be more mindful, meaning that they are more attuned to their own inner state and behaviour, including the ecological consequences of their actions. We can own fewer goods, but gain more satisfaction from them. We can reduce our carbon emissions, but have more fun. We can travel shorter distances, but enjoy life's journeys more. We can spend more time enjoying nature, and less time destroying it. We can eat local organic food, and feel healthier. We can live in small but comfortable houses that feel more like home. We can build denser neighborhoods that offer more public green space for exercising, playing, and relaxing. The key is to be better, not bigger.

The relationship between happiness and ecological footprints also holds true at the national level. Researchers who developed a "happy planet index" found that countries such as Bhutan and Costa Rica achieve high levels of happiness with small ecological footprints. The German ecological footprint is half that of the American footprint, yet the two countries have similar levels of happiness. As Mark Anielski, author of *The Economics of Happiness* concludes, "it is indeed possible for those of us from more affluent nations and communities to achieve a high quality of life with a smaller ecological footprint."

## MAKE A DIFFERENCE

THERE'S AN ANCIENT story about an old man who used to love walking near the ocean. He'd walk along the beach every morning. One day he saw a person moving like a dancer, bending, then wading into the waves with arms extended. It pleased him that someone would dance to the beauty of the day and the rhythm of the waves. As he got closer, he saw that it was a young girl. The girl wasn't dancing, but was reaching down to the sand, picking something up, and carrying it carefully out into the ocean.

He called out, "Good morning! What are you doing?"

The girl replied, "I'm returning starfish to the ocean."

"Why?"

"The sun is up and the tide is going out. If I don't rescue them, they'll be stranded on the beach and die."

"But there are miles upon miles of beach and starfish all along the way. What difference can you possibly make?"

The girl didn't answer right away. She bent down, picked up another starfish, and gently placed it in the sea. She watched a wave lift it high, and then, as it sank into the life-giving water, she turned to the man, smiled, and said, "I made a difference for that one."

He nodded and reflected for a moment. Then he bent down, picked up a starfish, and returned it to the sea.

The mutually beneficial relationship between personal and planetary well-being comes as no surprise to those who recognize that humans are part of nature, but runs contrary to the common misconception that reducing your footprint will somehow diminish your standard of living.

Your personal actions may seem like drops in the ocean, but everything you do has a ripple effect that multiplies your impact. When you turn off a light, you save up to three times as much energy as the light would have consumed. When you reduce your material consumption by a kilogram, you save up to 200 kilograms of natural resources and prevent up to 200 kilograms of waste and pollution. When you walk to work, ride a bicycle to the store, or enjoy a vacation closer to home, you prevent pollution, save natural resources, save money, improve your health, decrease wear and tear on roads, and boost your happiness. When you eat a meal of local organic food, you support the regional economy, decrease greenhouse gas emissions, protect wildlife habitat and soil quality, and feel healthy and happy. When you increase your home's energy efficiency you save money, take a bit of pressure off the planet, increase your level of comfort, and improve air quality. When you choose environmentally friendly products you send a signal to the market, and the market responds. When you vote for candidates based on their environmental platform, you start to change how governments operate. The ripple effect expands as you share your stories and experiences with family, friends, colleagues, and acquaintances. And remember that in a world of more than 6 billion people, each of us is a drop in the bucket, but with enough drops we can fill any bucket.

When we make changes at the individual level we are not alone. More and more people are discovering that environmentally responsible behavior is enriching, not impoverishing. Millions of people belong to international and national environmental groups, local green groups, and community sustainability groups. Thousands more join each day. As this wild and organic movement grows, it approaches what is known as a tipping point. Small changes that appear to have little or no effect on a system keep occurring until a critical mass is reached. Then one further small change "tips" the system and a large effect is observed. Exactly where a tipping point lies is unknown. Every person who joins the movement for a sustainable future brings us a little bit closer. Every builder working on zero energy or energy-plus homes brings us a little bit closer. Every farmer producing food sustainably brings us closer. Every business that shifts its practices and products towards cradle-to-cradle design brings us closer. Every government policy that rewards pro-environmental behavior and prohibits or penalizes ecologically destructive actions moves us towards the tipping point of the sustainability revolution.

Unfortunately, the natural world may also be teetering towards unknown tipping points, where climate change could accelerate or the rate of extinction could snowball. In this sense, we are in a race against time, making it imperative that we act now to put the brakes on our unsustainable levels of consumption, waste, and pollution.

If we can harness our knowledge, the deep reservoirs of human wisdom accumulated over millennia, and our unique gift of foresight, then we can achieve sustainability within one or two generations. Saving ourselves and countless other species from the brink of ecological disaster would be the greatest comeback of all time, outshining Team Canada's hockey victory in the 1972 Summit Series against the Soviet Union, won after early losses suggested there was no hope, Lance Armstrong's seven Tour de France championships, won after the cyclist battled testicular cancer, or the 1951 New York Giants baseball victory, won after the team overcame a thirteen-game deficit against archrival Brooklyn Dodgers. Today, Stanford ecologist Paul Ehrlich says there are a thousand ecological Pearl Harbors happening at once and we must mount an immediate and comprehensive response.

This book outlines, on the basis of the best scientific evidence, the most important steps you can take to reduce your ecological footprint. There's no expectation that you'll wake up tomorrow and change all the habits developed over your lifetime that contribute to environmental degradation. Striving for a sustainable lifestyle is like training for a marathon in that it requires dedication to develop healthy new habits. Every marathon begins with a first step. It's best to start slowly and gradually build on your successes. In the end you'll be a healthier, happier person. Be more mindful of the choices you make and their environmental implications. Think about where you choose to live, what you eat, how you travel, what you do for a living, what kind of stuff you buy, and how you exercise your democratic rights. Reflect on what makes you genuinely happy. Sign up for David Suzuki's Nature Challenge. Get out there and enjoy the natural world. Make your ecological footprint as small as possible.

Ultimately, you make the choices. As Dr. Seuss wrote in his 1971 classic *The Lorax*, "unless someone like you cares a whole awful lot, nothing is going to get better. It's not."

# Appendix:
# Background on the Global
# Environmental Crisis

*Human history becomes more and more
a race between education and catastrophe.*
H.G. WELLS

•  •  •

There are more than 6 billion people living on the Earth today, with the population expected to reach 9 billion by the middle of the twenty-first century. We are now the most numerous mammal on the planet. But unlike any other species, our technological prowess, appetite for resources, and global economy have made us a geological force. Agriculture, transportation, housing, industry, consumer goods, and day-to-day human activities are placing an unprecedented amount of pressure on the natural systems of the planet. The web of life, upon which our own future depends, is jeopardized by the crises of climate change, extinction, and toxic pollution.

## Climate Change

The Earth has a fever. Human activities are disrupting the planet's climate control system. Climate change is the most daunting environmental challenge ever confronted by humanity. The burning of coal, oil, and natural gas has pushed levels of carbon dioxide in the atmosphere to the highest levels in at least eight hundred thousand years. Agriculture and deforestation (for farms, ranches, timber, pulp and paper, and urban sprawl) are also major contributors to climate change.

The debate about the science of climate change is over. Eleven of the last twelve years are the hottest years on record (dating back to 1850). Oceans are warming to a depth of at least 3,000 meters (9,840 feet), surprising even climate scientists. Human emissions of greenhouse gases are changing the climate in ways that will result not only in warmer temperatures, but also heat waves, more frequent and intense storms and other extreme weather events, melting ice in the Arctic, Greenland, and the Antarctic, disappearing glaciers, melting permafrost, reduced flows in rivers, rising sea levels, floods, acidification of the oceans, and droughts.

The last time that the planet's polar regions were substantially warmer than today, about one hundred and twenty-five thousand years ago, sea levels rose by 4 to 6 meters (13 to 20 feet). This dramatic change, which would wreak terrible havoc around the world, could result from significant melting of the Greenland and West Antarctic ice sheets. While most scientists expect that this magnitude of sea level rise might take place over the course of several centuries, the nature of the climate system means that our actions today could make such a catastrophe inevitable. And there are frightening indications that the Greenland ice sheet is melting (and potentially sliding seaward) much more rapidly than anticipated. Carbon molecules emitted into the atmosphere stay there for a century or longer, so our generation is effectively lighting the fuse on a climate time bomb aimed at future generations, with no known means of defusing it.

In North America, the effects of climate change are already being felt. Forests are increasingly vulnerable to pests, disease, and wildfire, causing economic disruption of the forest industry and social dislocation in forest-dependent communities. Heavier spring runoff causes disruptive flooding. Lower summer river flows jeopardize agriculture and cause water stress. Heat waves are increasing in number, intensity, and duration. Extreme weather events such as Hurricane Katrina are becoming more common. Vectors of infectious diseases, such as West Nile virus, are changing. Levels of allergenic pollens are increasing, posing a health threat to tens of millions of people with asthma or other respiratory problems.

Although climate change is primarily caused by the wealthy industrialized nations, the bulk of adverse health effects will be borne by developing nations that are more vulnerable and lack adequate resources to adapt. Climate change already causes an estimated one hundred and fifty thousand deaths and 5 million illnesses per year. The World Health Organization projects a doubling of these figures by 2030. Fewer deaths from cold exposure in northern nations will be outweighed by the increased frequency of cardiorespiratory diseases and the increased burden of diarrheal disease in developing nations.

Tens of millions of people may be displaced from their homes by flooding, spawning an unprecedented wave of environmental refugees. More than a billion people will face chronic water shortages as precipitation patterns change and water supplies stored in glaciers and snow packs decline. Malaria is already spreading its deadly reach to higher elevations in Africa, threatening previously safe populations. Increased drought is projected to have the greatest impact on regions of Africa that are already experiencing significant levels of malnutrition. Crop yields in parts of Africa may fall by as much as 50%. The shift towards biofuels in wealthy nations threatens to exacerbate nutritional deficiencies in poorer nations as crops that once fed people are used to make fuel for machines, reducing food supplies and driving food prices up.

Between 1970 and 2004, global greenhouse gas emissions increased 70%. Despite the international climate change agreements negotiated during the 1990s, experts predict that emissions will rise 55% to 90% by 2030. Fossil fuels still provide more than 80% of the total global energy supply, a dominant position that is not expected to change by 2030 despite efforts to reduce greenhouse gas emissions.

## Disappearing Diversity

Biological diversity—the richness of life measured at the species, eco-system, or genetic level—is disappearing more rapidly than at any time since the extinction of the dinosaurs 65 million years ago. Scientists esti-mate that species are going extinct at a rate that is one hundred to one thousand times faster than normal and fear that the pace of extinctions will accelerate in the decades ahead. Again it is human activity that is the primary cause of the problem. The combined impact of overex-ploitation, habitat destruction, climate change, invasive species, ozone depletion, and toxic pollution is taking a terrible toll on ecosystems and species.

One in three amphibians, one in four mammals, and one in eight bird species are threatened with extinction over the next century. Spe-cies teetering on the brink of disappearing forever include some of our closest living relatives—orangutans, chimpanzees, and mountain goril-las. The living planet index, created by several different institutions, including the Zoological Society of London and the World Wildlife Fund, tracks populations of more than thirteen hundred vertebrate species—mammals, birds, fish, amphibians, and reptiles—living in ter-restrial, marine, and freshwater ecosystems. Between 1970 and 2007, the living planet index fell by almost one-third. According to the World Wildlife Fund, "this global trend suggests that we are degrading natural ecosystems at a rate unprecedented in human history."

The UN's Millennium Ecosystem Assessment, an exhaustive analysis of the state of life on Earth prepared by more than thirteen hundred experts, concluded that "Human activity is putting such strain on the natural functions of the Earth that the ability of the planet's ecosys-tems to sustain future generations can no longer be taken for granted." Approximately one-quarter of the Earth's land surface has been trans-formed from wild to cultivated systems. Tens of billions of chickens, pigs, and cattle are being raised to feed humans, using land that was once wildlife habitat. Many ecosystems, from tall grass prairies to redwood forests, from coastal mangroves to wetlands, have been almost completely converted into pasture, farmland, tree farms, shrimp farms, and suburbia. At least 60% of the world's natural resources and life-supporting ecosystems are in decline.

As recently as the 1950s, students were taught that oceans offered an inexhaustible supply of protein. Today, despite the fact that oceans cover close to three-quarters of the Earth's surface, marine ecosystems are among the most depleted on the planet. Populations of large predatory fishes—bluefin tuna, swordfish, sharks—have declined by more than 90%. Some scientists predict that if current fishing practices continue, all commercially targeted fish species will suffer population collapses by 2048. As a result, the oceans will be unable to contribute to feeding a growing human population, and marine ecosystems will suffer a severe decrease in their ability to resist diseases, cope with invasive species, filter pollutants, and rebound from stresses.

The impacts of climate change on biodiversity could be devastating. Scientists are already observing earlier bird migrations and egg laying in the spring. Bird movement and chick hatching are exquisitely dependent on cycles of food and predation that are themselves disrupted by climate change. As well, plants and animals are found to be moving towards the poles and up the sides of mountains to stay within their optimum temperature range. Experts anticipate major losses of coastal wetlands, coral reefs, mangrove forests, tropical forests, and other vital ecosystems. Polar bears may disappear from the wild and be found only in zoos. Thousands of other animal and plant species will go extinct, with estimates of about 30% globally. Tropical rainforests will be particularly hard hit.

### Toxic Pollution

Toxic industrial and agricultural chemicals now contaminate the bodies of every single person in the world. We can't escape the toxic discharges of industries because we're exposed to hundreds, if not thousands of hazardous substances through the air we breathe, the water we drink, the food we eat, and the myriad consumer products we use. Tests examining the blood and urine of Americans, Canadians, Europeans, and Australians, urban and rural, young and old, find heavy metals, pesticides, flame retardants, stain repellants, and PCBs, many of which didn't even exist a century ago. Even the cord blood of newborn infants in the U.S. contains over two hundred industrial chemicals. These studies remind us of the fundamental connection between humans and the environment. Despite our technological wizardry and the widespread perception that humans are separate from nature, the fact remains that what we do to the planet, we do to ourselves.

Total releases of toxic chemicals into our environment by large industries in the U.S. and Canada are astronomical, measured in the tens of billions of kilograms annually. American and Canadian industries spew over 60 million kilograms (132 million pounds) of known or suspected carcinogens into the air annually, including styrene, benzene, and formaldehyde. They dump over 700,000 kilograms (1.5 million pounds) of known or suspected carcinogens—including lead, chloroform, and carbon tetrachloride—into rivers, lakes, and other water bodies every year. More than 50 million kilograms (110 million pounds) of chemicals that cause developmental or reproductive problems—including toluene, mercury, and carbon disulfide—are discharged into the environment annually. These are mind-boggling statistics, yet the databases from which these figures are derived cover only a small subset of the toxic chemicals used in large volumes by North American industry, and are unaudited figures reported by corporations. Agricultural runoff, urban runoff, small and medium-sized businesses, and motor vehicles release billions of additional kilograms of toxic substances into our environment. Most kitchen, laundry, workshop, and medicine shelves hold dozens of harmful chemicals that may end up in sewers or landfills. Despite all of the promises and press releases from government and industry about going green, the fact remains that we still treat the environment like an infinite garbage dump.

People are paying a price for this recklessness. Exposure to environmental hazards is a major cause of death and disease around the world. According to the World Health Organization, one-quarter of the death and illness globally is attributable to environmental problems. Exposure to environmental contaminants can cause cancer, harm immune systems, cause birth defects, prevent the normal development of children, interfere with the respiratory, cardiovascular, reproductive, hormonal, and nervous systems, and cause neurological diseases. Children are particularly vulnerable. One-third of children's illnesses and injuries in Europe are caused by environmental factors.

The health toll inflicted by environmental hazards includes close to 2 million deaths annually in poor countries caused by diarrheal diseases linked to unsafe drinking water and inadequate sanitation facilities. Indoor air pollution, primarily from burning fuels for cooking and heating, kills close to 2 million people per year. Outdoor air pollution caused by motor vehicles, energy generation, and industry causes another million deaths annually. Exposure to lead causes hundreds of thousands of deaths globally each year, and harms the development of at least one-third of the world's children. Poisonings caused by exposure to pesticides and other toxic chemicals are estimated to kill 355,000 people annually. In total, preventable deaths caused by environmental hazards kill at least 15,000 human beings per day, or 625 people per hour, or 5 people in the time it takes you to read this paragraph. Most of the casualties are children.

## Good News

Not all environmental trends are negative. The greatest environmental success story in recent memory is the protection of the Earth's ozone layer. The production and use of CFCs and other ozone-depleting chemicals during the twentieth century posed a serious threat to the future of life. The ozone layer performs the function of absorbing much of the harmful ultraviolet radiation streaming to Earth from the Sun. In the late 1980s, scientists were concerned that if the thinning of the ozone layer worsened as projected, people would scarcely be able to venture outdoors in certain latitudes without putting themselves at risk of skin cancer. Thankfully, the implementation of an international agreement called the Montreal Protocol on Substances That Deplete the Ozone Layer caused a decline of more than 95% in the use and release of these chemicals in North America and more than 80% globally. The agreement put the greatest burden of reduction on the industrialized world, requiring rich nations to act first. Twenty years after the Montreal Protocol, in 2007, governments agreed to accelerate the elimination of the remaining ozone-depleting chemicals. Experts anticipate that the ozone layer will gradually heal itself over the course of the next century.

Big, beautiful areas of vital importance to the conservation of biological diversity have been set aside as parks and wildlife refuges all around the world, protected from mining, logging, and other destructive industrial activities. Hundreds of millions of hectares have been saved, including spectacular ecological treasures such as Brazil's Central Amazon Conservation Complex (including Jau National Park), China's Three Parallel Rivers of Yunnan, the Great Barrier Reef, the Galapagos Islands, and parks spanning the Rocky Mountains from Yellowstone to the Yukon.

Society is making progress in phasing out the use of some of the most deadly toxic chemicals ever created. The Stockholm Convention on Persistent Organic Pollutants targets the so-called dirty dozen, including dioxins, furans, and PCBs, for elimination.

Most countries have banned the use of leaded gasoline, a product that damaged the development of millions of children around the world during the twentieth century. International negotiations are underway to stop the use of other harmful substances including mercury and a group of flame retardants called PBDEs that are rapidly accumulating in wildlife and women's breast milk. In western nations, levels of most air pollutants have declined and great strides have been made in addressing the problem of acid rain.

The good news does not end there. Production of wind and solar energy is soaring and further technological breakthroughs are on the horizon. Sales of local and organic food are blossoming. Sales of highly efficient hybrid vehicles are racing. All of these environmentally friendly options are growing at far faster rates than their conventional counterparts. But these trends, although positive, are outweighed by the bleak news about climate change, declining biodiversity, and toxic pollution. As Ronald Wright says in A *Short History of Progress*, "Now is our last chance to get the future right."

# Resources

•   •   •

## CHAPTER 1 | *Help Wanted: Join the Sustainability Revolution*
READ

Benyus, J. *Biomimicry: Innovation Inspired by Nature*. New York: William Morrow, 1997.

Boyd, D.R. *Sustainability Within a Generation: A New Vision for Canada*. Vancouver: David Suzuki Foundation, 2004.

Bradford, T. *Solar Revolution: The Economic Transformation of the Global Energy Industry*. Cambridge: MIT Press, 2006.

Brower, M., and W. Leon. *The Consumer's Guide to Effective Environmental Choices: Practical Advice from the Union of Concerned Scientists*. New York: Three Rivers Press, 1999.

Hawken, P., A. Lovins, and L.H. Lovins. *Natural Capitalism: Creating the Next Industrial Revolution*. Boston: Little, Brown and Company, 1999.

McDonough, W., and M. Braungart. *Cradle to Cradle: Remaking the Way We Make Things*. New York: North Point Press, 2002.

Suzuki, D., and H. Dressel. *Good News for a Change: How Everyday People Are Helping the Planet*. Vancouver: Greystone, 2003.

Turner, C. *The Geography of Hope: A Tour of the World We Need*. Toronto: Random House, 2007.

Wackernagel, M., and W. Rees. *Our Ecological Footprint: Reducing Human Impact on the Earth*. Gabriola, BC: New Society Publishers, 1996.

SURF

David Suzuki Foundation: www.davidsuzuki.org
Ecogeek: www.ecogeek.org
Global Footprint Network: www.globalfootprint.org
GreenBlue Institute: www.greenblue.org
McDonough Braungart Design Chemistry: www.mbdc.com
Net-zero Energy Home Coalition: www.netzeroenergyhome.ca
One Planet Living: www.oneplanetliving.org
Redefining Progress: www.myfootprint.org
Sweden's Ministry of the Environment: www.sweden.gov.se/sb/d/2066
Tesla Motors: www.teslamotors.com
Treehugger: www.treehugger.com
World Wildlife Fund: www.wwf.org
Zero Waste International Alliance: www.zwia.org

CHAPTER 2 | *Home Smart Home*

READ

Consumer Reports. *Complete Guide to Reducing Energy Costs.* Yonkers,
NY: Consumer's Union of the United States, 2006.

Gauley, W., and J. Koeller. *Maximum Performance Testing of Popular
Toilet Models: A Cooperative Canadian and American Project.* 9th ed.
Mississauga, ON: Veritec Consulting, 2007. (Available at www.cwwa.
ca or www.cuwcc.org)

Johnston, J., and K. Master. *Green Remodeling: Changing the World One
Room at a Time.* Gabriola, BC: New Society Publishers, 2004.

Scheckel, P. *The Home Energy Diet: How to Save Money by Making Your
House Energy-smart.* Gabriola, BC: New Society Publishers, 2005.

Stoyke, G. *The Carbon Buster's Home Energy Handbook: Slowing
Climate Change and Saving Money.* Gabriola, BC: New Society
Publishers, 2007.

Thorne Amann, J., and A. Wilson. *Consumer Guide to Home Energy
Savings: Save Money, Save the Earth.* 9th ed. Gabriola, BC: New
Society Publishers, 2007.

Venolia, C., and K. Lerner. *Natural Remodeling for the Not-So-Green House: Bringing Your Home into Harmony with Nature*. Asheville, NC: Lark Books. 2006.

Vickers, A. *Handbook of Water Use and Conservation: Homes, Landscapes, Businesses, Industries, Farms*. Amherst, MA: WaterPlow Press, 2001.

Wilson, A. *Your Green Home: A Guide to Planning a Healthy, Environmentally Friendly New Home*. Gabriola, BC: New Society Publishers, 2006.

Wilson, A., and M. Piepcorn, eds. *Green Building Products: The Greenspec Guide to Residential Building Materials*. 2nd ed. Gabriola, BC: New Society Publishers, 2006.

## WATCH

*The End of Suburbia*
*Escape from Suburbia: Beyond the American Dream*

## SURF | ENERGY AND WATER CONSERVATION

Alliance to Save Energy: www.energyhog.org
American Council for an Energy-Efficient Economy: www.aceee.org/Consumer/consumer.htm
Canada Mortgage and Housing Corporation: www.cmhc.ca
Home Energy Magazine: www.homeenergy.org
Natural Home Magazine: www.naturalhomemagazine.com
U.S. Office of Energy Efficiency and Renewable Energy: www.eere.energy.gov
Water Conserve (portal and search engine): www.waterconserve.org
Water—Use It Wisely: www.wateruseitwisely.com

## SURF | GREEN BUILDINGS

Canada Green Building Council: www.cagbc.org
Green Building Council of Australia: www.gbcaus.org
Greenbuilding (E.U.): www.eu-greenbuilding.org

Light House Sustainable Building Centre: www.sustainablebuilding
   centre.com
U.S. Green Building Council: www.usgbc.org

SURF | GREEN BUILDING SUPPLIES
AND HOME PRODUCTS

Environmental Home Center and Environmental Building Supplies:
   www.ecohaus.com
Green Depot: www.GreenDepot.com
GreenSpec Directory: www.buildinggreen.com
Healthy Home Store: www.thehealthiesthome.com

CHAPTER 3 | *Food for Thought: Eating a Planet-friendly Diet*

READ
Berry, W. The Pleasures of Eating. In *What Are People For?* New York:
   North Point Press, 1990.
Davis, B., and V. Melina. *Becoming Vegan: The Complete Guide to
   Adopting a Healthy Plant-based Diet.* Summertown, TN: Book
   Publishing Company, 2000.
Goodall, J. *Harvest for Hope: A Guide to Mindful Eating.* New York:
   Warner Wellness, 2005.
Kingsolver, B., C. Kingsolver, and S.L. Hogg. *Animal, Vegetable,
   Miracle: A Year of Food Life.* New York: Harper Collins, 2007.
Lappe, F.M., and A. Lappe. *Hope's Edge: The Next Diet for a Small
   Planet.* New York: Tarcher, 2003.
Melina, V., and B. Davis. *The New Becoming Vegetarian: The Essential
   Guide to a Healthy Diet.* 2nd ed. Summertown, TN: Healthy Living
   Publications, 2003.
Menzel, P., and F. D'Aluisio. *Hungry Planet: What the World Eats.*
   Berkeley: Material World Books and Ten Speed Press, 2005.
Nabhan, G.P. *Coming Home to Eat: The Pleasures and Politics of Local
   Food.* New York: W.W. Norton, 2001.

Nestle, M. *What to Eat.* New York: North Point Press, 2006.

Petrini, C. *Slow Food Nation: Why Our Food Should Be Good, Clean, and Fair.* New York: Rizzoli Ex Libris, 2007.

Pollan, M. *The Omnivore's Dilemma: A Natural History of Four Meals.* New York: Penguin, 2006.

——. *In Defense of Food: An Eater's Manifesto.* New York: Penguin, 2008.

Robbins, J. *The Food Revolution: How Your Diet Can Help Save Your Life and Our World.* Newburyport, MA: Conari Press, 2001.

Safina, C. *Song for a Blue Ocean: Encounters Along the World's Coasts and Beneath the Seas.* New York: Henry Holt, 1997.

·Singer, P., and J. Mason. *The Way We Eat: Why Our Food Choices Matter.* New York: Rodale Press, 2006.

Smith, A., and J.B. MacKinnon. *The 100-Mile Diet: A Year of Local Eating.* Toronto: Random House, 2007.

Wood, R. *The New Whole Foods Encyclopedia: A Comprehensive Resource for Healthy Eating.* New York: Penguin, 1999.

WATCH

*Babe*
*The Fight for True Farming*
*The Future of Food*
*The Global Banquet: Politics of Food*
*The Meatrix* (an Internet classic)
*Our Daily Bread*
*The Real Dirt on Farmer John*
*Run, Chicken Run*
*Super Size Me*

SURF

100-Mile Diet: www.100milediet.org
The Eat Well Guide: www.eatwellguide.org

The Edible Schoolyard: www.edibleschoolyard.org

Farmfolk/Cityfolk Society: www.ffcf.bc.ca

Food Routes Network: www.foodroutes.org

Gardening: www.containergardeningtips.com, www.weekend
gardener.net/vegetable-gardening-tips/starting-garden-050705.htm,
www.gardeningknowhow.com/vegetable/organic-vegetable-
gardens.htm

Grass-fed meat and dairy products: www.eatwild.com

International Slow Food Movement: www.slowfood.com

National Farm to School Program: www.farmtoschool.org

Organic Consumers Association: www.organicconsumers.org

Organic seeds and foods: www.seedsofchange.com

Stop Global Warming. . . one bite at a time: www.coolyourdiet.org

Sustainable food: www.heritagefoodsusa.com

CHAPTER 4 | *Traveling Light*

READ

Alvord, K. *Divorce Your Car: Ending the Love Affair with the Automobile.*
Gabriola, BC: New Society Publishers, 2000.

Balish, C. *How to Live Well Without Owning a Car: Save Money,
Breathe Easier, and Get More Mileage Out of Life.* Berkeley: Ten
Speed Press, 2006.

Bradsher, K. *High and Mighty: SUVs—The World's Most Dangerous
Vehicles and How They Got That Way.* New York: Public
Affairs, 2002.

Crawford, J.H. *Carfree Cities.* Utrecht: International Books, 2002.

Doyle, J. *Taken for a Ride: Detroit's Big Three and the Politics of
Pollution.* New York: Four Walls Eight Windows, 2000.

Ghent, R. *Cutting Your Car Use: Save Money, Be Healthy, Be Green!*
Gabriola, BC: New Society Publishers, 2006.

Holtz Kay, J. *Asphalt Nation: How the Automobile Took Over America
and How We Can Take It Back.* Berkeley: University of California
Press, 1998.

Romm, J.J. *The Hype about Hydrogen: Fact and Fiction in the Race to Save the Climate.* Washington, DC: Island Press, 2005.

Sloman, L. *Car Sick: Solutions for Our Car-Addicted Culture.* Totnes, Devon: Green Books, 2006.

Tamminen, T. *Lives per Gallon: The True Cost of Our Oil Addiction.* Washington, DC: Island Press, 2006.

Yost, N. *The Essential Hybrid Car Handbook: A Buyer's Guide.* Guilford, CT: Lyons Press, 2006.

WATCH

*Who Killed the Electric Car?*

SURF

American Council for an Energy Efficient Economy's Green Book: www.greenercars.org

Canadian Telework Association: www.ivc.ca/cta

Eco-driving: www.ecodriving.org

Green Car Journal: www.greencar.com

Videoconferencing basics: www.officevideoconferencing.com

Walking schoolbus programs: www.walkingschoolbus.org

CHAPTER 5 | *Less Stuff: The Zero Waste Challenge*

READ

Campbell, S. *Let It Rot: The Gardener's Guide to Composting.* 3rd ed. North Adams, MA: Storey Publishing, 1998.

de Graaf, J., D. Wann, and T.H. Naylor. *Affluenza: The All-Consuming Epidemic.* San Francisco: Berrett Koehler, 2005.

Dodd, D.L. *Home Safe Home: Protecting Yourself and Your Family from Everyday Toxics and Harmful Household Products.* New York: Tarcher, 2005.

Dominguez, J., and V. Robin. *Your Money or Your Life: Transforming Your Relationship with Money and Achieving Financial Independence.* New York: Penguin, 1999.

Elgin, D. *Voluntary Simplicity: Toward a Way of Life That Is Outwardly Simple, Inwardly Rich.* New York: Harper, 1998.

Ellis, B.W., and F.M. Bradley. *The Organic Gardener's Handbook of Natural Insect and Disease Control: A Complete Problem-Solving Guide to Keeping Your Garden and Yard Healthy Without Chemicals.* New York: Rodale Press, 1996.

Ettlinger, S. *Twinkie, Deconstructed: My Journey to Discover How the Ingredients Found in Processed Foods Are Grown, Mined (Yes, Mined), and Manipulated into What America Eats.* New York: Hudson Street Press, 2007.

Griffin, S. *CancerSmart Guide for Consumers 3.0.* Vancouver: Labour and Environmental Alliance Society, 2007.

Hollender, J., G. David, M. Hollender, and R. Doyle. *Naturally Clean: The Seventh Generation Guide to Safe and Healthy Non-toxic Cleaning.* Gabriola, BC: New Society Publishers, 2006.

Klein, N. *No Logo: No Space, No Choice, No Jobs.* New York: Picador, 2002.

Lasn, K. *Culture Jam: How to Reverse America's Suicidal Consumer Binge, and Why We Must.* New York: Harper, 2000.

Rivoli, P. *The Travels of a T-Shirt in the Global Economy: An Economist Examines the Markets, Power, and Politics of World Trade.* Hoboken, NJ: Wiley, 2006.

Royte, E. *Garbage Land: On the Secret Trail of Trash.* New York: Back Bay Books, 2006.

Rubin, C. *How to Get Your Lawn and Garden Off Drugs: A Basic Guide to Pesticide-free Gardening in North America.* 2nd ed. Madiera Park, BC: Harbour Publishing, 2003.

Ryan, J.C. *Seven Wonders: Everyday Things for a Healthier Planet.* Seattle: Sierra Club Books, 1999.

Ryan, J.C., and A.T. Durning. *Stuff: The Secret Lives of Everyday Things.* Seattle: Northwest Environment Watch, 1997.

Sandbeck, E. *Organic Housekeeping.* New York: Scribners, 2006.

*The Story of Stuff*: www.storyofstuff.com

SURF

Alternative Gift Registry: www.alternativegiftregistry.org
American Lung Association's Health House: www.healthhouse.org
Be, Live, Buy Different—Make a Difference: www.ibuydifferent.org
Better Basics for the Home: Simple Solutions for Less Toxic Living:
    www.betterbasics.com
The Center for a New American Dream: www.Newdream.org
Certified green cleaning products: www.newdream.org/cleanschools/
    safelist.php
Common household products and ingredients: www.Household
    Products.nlm.nih.gov
Environmental Health Association of Nova Scotia's Guide to Less Toxic
    Products: www.lesstoxicguide.ca
Grassroots Recycling Network: www.grrn.org
National Geographic's The Green Guide: www.thegreenguide.com
No Impact Man: www.noimpactman.com
The Simple Living Network: www.Simpleliving.net

**CHAPTER 6 | *Citizen Green***

READ

Ausenda, F. *Green Volunteers: The World Guide to Voluntary Work in
    Nature Conservation*. New York: Universe, 2007.
Environmental Careers Organization. *The ECO Guide to Careers That
    Make a Difference: Environmental Work for a Sustainable World*.
    Washington, DC: Island Press, 2004.
Environmental Jobs Network. *Guide to Environmental Careers in
    Australia*. Melbourne: EJN, 2005.
Fasulo, M., and P. Walker. *Careers in the Environment*. 3rd ed. New
    York: McGraw-Hill, 2007.

Goodall, J. *Reason for Hope: A Spiritual Journey.* New York: Grand Central, 2000.

Jones, E., R. Haehfler, and B. Johnson. *The Better World Handbook: Small Changes That Make a Big Difference.* Gabriola, BC: New Society Publishers, 2007.

Maathai, W. *Unbowed: A Memoir.* New York: Knopf, 2006.

May, E. *How to Save the Planet in Your Spare Time.* Toronto: Key Porter, 2006.

Steffen, A., ed. *Worldchanging: A User's Guide to the 21st Century.* New York: Harry N. Abrams, 2006.

Suzuki, D. *David Suzuki: The Autobiography.* Vancouver: Greystone, 2006.

Suzuki, D., and H. Dressel. *Good News for a Change: How Everyday People Are Helping the Planet.* Vancouver: Greystone, 2003.

Yunus, M. *Banker to the Poor: Micro-Lending and the Battle Against World Poverty.* New York: Public Affairs, 2003.

WATCH

*China Syndrome*
*A Civil Action*
*Erin Brockovich*
*Silkwood*

SURF | POLITICAL ACTION

Fair Vote Canada: www.fairvotecanada.org
FairVote (The Center for Voting and Democracy): www.fairvote.org
Presidential Climate Action Project: www.climateactionproject.org
Sierra Club (U.S.): www.sierraclub.org
Sierra Club of Canada: www.sierraclub.ca

SURF | CAREERS IN THE ENVIRONMENTAL FIELD

Action Without Borders: www.idealist.org
Environmental Career Opportunities: www.ecojobs.com

Environmental Careers (U.K.): www.environmentcareers.org.uk
Environmental Careers Organization (Canada): www.eco.ca
Environmental Jobs and Careers: www.ecoemploy.com
Environmental Jobs Network (Australia):
   www.environmentaljobs.com.au
GreenBiz.com: www.greenbiz.com

SURF | ETHICAL INVESTING
Australia: www.responsibleinvestment.org
Canada: www.socialinvestment.ca
U.K.: www.uksif.org
U.S.: www.socialinvest.org

CHAPTER 7 | *Smaller Footprint, Bigger Smile*
READ

Anielski, M. *The Economics of Happiness: Building Genuine Wealth.*
   Gabriola, BC: New Society Publishers, 2007.
Gladwell, M. *The Tipping Point: How Little Things Can Make a Big
   Difference.* Boston: Little, Brown and Company, 2002.
Hawken, P. *Blessed Unrest: How the Largest Movement in the World
   Came into Being and Why No One Saw It Coming.* New York:
   Viking, 2007.
Kasser, T. *The High Price of Materialism.* Cambridge: MIT Press, 2002.
McKibben, B. *Deep Economy: The Wealth of Communities and the
   Durable Future.* New York: Times Books, 2007.
Layard, R. *Happiness: Lessons from a New Science.* London:
   Allen Lane, 2005.
Louv, R. *Last Child in the Woods: Saving Our Children from Nature-
   deficit Disorder.* Chapel Hill, NC: Algonquin, 2005.
Marks, N., S. Abdallah, A. Simms, and S. Thompson. *The (un)Happy
   Planet Index: An Index of Human Well-being and Environmental
   Impact.* London: New Economics Foundation, 2006.

Nettle, D. *Happiness: The Science Behind Your Smile*. Oxford: Oxford University Press, 2005.

Putnam, R.D. *Bowling Alone: The Collapse and Revival of American Community*. New York: Simon & Schuster, 2000.

Suzuki, D., and A. McConnell. *The Sacred Balance: Rediscovering Our Place in Nature*. Vancouver: Greystone, 1997.

WATCH

*The 11th Hour*
*An Inconvenient Truth*

SURF

David Suzuki Foundation: www.davidsuzuki.org
New Economics Foundation: www.neweconomics.org

# Index

ecology, 2–3
Edible Schoolyard program, 61
education, 134–35, 140
Ehrlich, Paul, 146
Einstein, Albert, 2
electric bicycles, 80
electric cars, 14, 85
electricity (*See also* appliances; house-
     holds): consumption, 6; and house-
     hold use, 23–26, 28–31, 33; for hybrids
     and electric cars, 85; reductions in,
     131–32; from renewable resources,
     12–13, 35, 129
energy audits, 25–28
energy consumption: and carbon
     dioxide emissions, 7; and ecological
     footprint, 3–5; and electricity, 6; of
     households, 21–22, 23–24, 25, 28; of
     manufacturing, 92–93; tips for reduc-
     ing, 95–99, 102–9; of transportation,
     77; and waste, 93–95
energy conversion loss, 24–25
energy efficiency: in appliances, 28–31;
     and audits, 25–28; in electricity use,
     131–32; at home, 24–26
energy reduction: in agriculture, 15;
     amount needed for survival, 94; in
     appliances, 19–20, 28–31; benefits of,
     110, 145; in building homes, 13–14; in
     cars, 14; in cooling, 26, 27; and eco-
     logical literacy, 135; and energy audits,
     25–28; and food, 14, 30, 80; in heat-
     ing, 26, 27, 30, 35; and home location,
     22–23; from improved efficiency,
     24–31, 131–32; in lighting, 17–18,
     33–34; and manufacturing, 16, 17;
     from smart growth, 133; tips for reduc-
     ing consumption, 95–99, 102–9; in
     waste, 14–15; in water heating, 31–33

Energy Star program, 29, 100
Environmental Choice programs,
     100, 101
environmental damage (*See also*
     ecological footprint; greenhouse
     gases; pollution): climate change,
     148–50, 152; disappearing diversity
     of species, 151–52; and food system,
     45–46, 50, 52, 53–54, 57–58, 59, 61;
     by individuals, 18; from meat-eating,
     46, 50, 52; toxic pollution, 152–54
environmental movement, 9–10
environmental standards programs, 29,
     43, 100, 101, 131
ethanol, 89–90
extreme weather events, 149–50

fair-trade goods, 58
farmers' markets, 55–56
farming, 15, 36, 46, 55, 59–60
feed-in tariffs, 129
fish/fishing: buying local, 55; dietary
     choice of, 50, 51; environmental
     impact of, 46, 152; ethics of, 52, 53;
     starfish story, 144
floods, 149, 150
food, 45–70; and bottled water, 67–69;
     cost of, 61; dietary choices, 47–53,
     62–63, 69–70; eating more slowly
     and less, 64–66; and energy reduc-
     tion, 14, 30, 80; environmental
     effect of, 45–46, 50, 52, 53–54,
     57–58, 59, 61; and government
     promotion, 133–34; and health,
     45–47, 48, 50, 51, 52, 66, 133–34;
     and health care, 65–66; and locali-
     zation, 54–58; organic, 50, 56,
     57, 58, 59–62; and reading labels,
     65; shipping of, 53–54, 61; and

households, 21–44; and appliances, 28–31; and energy audits, 25–28; energy consumption of, 21–22, 23–24, 25, 28; and energy efficiency, 24–26, 28–31; and green building, 43–44; greenhouse gases from, 14, 21, 31, 32, 33; importance of location, 22–23; and lighting, 33–34; size of, 21–22; and transportation, 74; using renewable energy, 13–14; water conservation, 36–42; and water heating, 31–33
hybrid vehicles, 84–85, 86, 87
hydrogen fuel, 12, 14, 88–89

ice sheets, melting of, 149, 150
incentive programs, 40.
    *See also* tax incentives
infrastructure, 73
insulation, 26
Internet, 103, 105, 109, 122
investment, socially responsible, 126–27

Jackson, Wes, 15

Kingsolver, Barbara, 58

label reading, 65, 99–101
land conservation, 116–17, 123
landfills, 102, 108
landscaping, 27, 38, 39
land use, 133
lawns, 38, 39
League of Conservation Voters (LCV), 116
leaks, in homes, 26, 37, 39, 41
LEDs (light-emitting diodes), 33, 34
LEED standards, 43
lifestyle changes, 20

light-emitting diodes (LEDs), 33, 34
lighting, 17–18, 24, 25, 33–34
liquefied petroleum gas (LPG), 89
living planet index, 151
localization, 54–58, 97

Maathai, Wangari, 112–13
MacKinnon, J.B., 58
Mandela, Nelson, 113
manufacturing/manufactured goods: cradle-to-cradle approach, 15–17, 100, 104, 110, 130; and energy consumption, 92–93; and energy efficiency appliances, 31; and environmental standards, 131; and health, 97; reading labels on, 99–101; recycling, 15–17, 96–97, 99, 105, 129–30; and toxic substances, 68; and waste, 14, 16–17; ways to cut down consuming, 94–99, 102–9
mass transit, 78, 83, 133
materialism. *See* consumerism
McDonough, William, 15–16, 93
meat eating: environmental impact of, 46, 50, 52; ethics of, 52–53; and free range livestock, 48, 50; and health, 52; tips for reducing, 47–48
media, 1, 92, 98, 117, 134
mercury, 33–34, 50
methane gas, 108
microcredit programs, 127
Millennium Ecosystem Assessment, 151
Montreal Protocol, 155

Nabhan, Gary Paul, 58
natural resources, 94, 106.
    *See also* fossil fuels
nature, 2–3, 139–40
Nike, 17

oceans, 149, 152
OECD (Organization for Economic
    Co-operation and Development), 94
office equipment, 16
offsets, carbon, 90–91
oil, 12–13, 82, 83, 86
Oliver, Jamie, 61
organic food, 50, 56, 57, 58, 59–62
Organization for Economic
    Co-operation and Development
    (OECD), 94
ozone layer, 154–55

packaging, waste from, 108
paper, 20, 106, 107
pesticides, 59, 60, 122, 128, 130
plastic bags, 103–4
plastics, recycling, 107
plug-in hybrids, 85
pollution: and food system, 46; from
    ordinary consumption, 93–94;
    success stories in fighting, 154–55;
    taxes on, 132; from transportation, 72,
    82, 86, 89; as worldwide environmen-
    tal concern, 7, 152–54
propane, 89
proportional representation, 115–16
protein, 48, 50
public transit, 78, 83, 133

quality of life, 20, 23, 98, 139–41,
    143–44

rainwater harvesting, 39
rebates, 40, 84, 87
recreation, 92, 98
recycling: appliances, 30–31, 106, 107;
    cans, 19, 107; and combating waste,
    96, 106–8; laws for, 109, 110–11; light

bulbs, 34; manufactured products,
    15–17, 96–97, 99, 105, 129–30
refrigerators, 19, 28, 29, 30–31
renewable energy: European plans for,
    12–13; and green power, 35; in house-
    holds, 13–14; laws for, 12, 129; plans
    for, 128–29; solar power, 11–12, 13–14,
    32, 125, 129, 156; and subsidies, 132–33;
    wind power, 12–13, 125, 129, 156
repairing manufactured products, 105–6
retrofits. See energy audits
roof gardens, 27
Roy, Dick, 95
Roy, Jeanne, 95

Salatin, Joel, 15
salmon, 51
Schwarzenegger, Arnold, 129
Scientific Certification Systems
    (SCS), 101
scooters, 80
seafood, 50, 51
sea levels, rise of, 149
Shaw, George Bernard, 53
ships, 81
shopping, 80, 92
showers, 37, 38, 41
slow food movement, 64
smart growth, 133
Smith, Alisa, 58
socially responsible investing, 126–27
social problems, 141
solar power, 11–12, 13–14, 32, 125,
    129, 156
space race, 8
species extinction, 151–52
starfish story, 144
Stockholm Convention on Persistent
    Organic Pollutants, 155

*The Last Great Sea* by Terry Glavin

*Northern Wild* by David R. Boyd, ed.

*Greenhouse* by Gale E. Christianson

*Vanishing Halo* by Daniel Gawthrop

*The Sacred Balance: Rediscovering Our Place in Nature*
by David Suzuki, Amanda McConnell, and Adrienne Mason

*Dead Reckoning* by Terry Glavin

*Delgamuukw* by Stan Persky

## DAVID SUZUKI FOUNDATION CHILDREN'S TITLES

*Salmon Forest* by David Suzuki and Sarah Ellis;
illustrated by Sheena Lott

*You are the Earth* by David Suzuki and Kathy Vanderlinden

*Eco-Fun* by David Suzuki and Kathy Vanderlinden

*There's a Barnyard in My Bedroom* by David Suzuki;
illustrated by Eugenie Fernandes

## DAVID SUZUKI FOUNDATION

The David Suzuki Foundation works through science and education to protect the diversity of nature and our quality of life, now and for the future.

With a goal of achieving sustainability within a generation, the Foundation collaborates with scientists, business and industry, academia, government and non-governmental organizations. We seek the best research to provide innovative solutions that will help build a clean, competitive economy that does not threaten the natural services that support all life.

The Foundation is a federally registered independent charity, which is supported with the help of over 50,000 individual donors across Canada and around the world.

We invite you to become a member. For more information on how you can support our work, please contact us:

The David Suzuki Foundation
219–2211 West 4th Avenue
Vancouver, BC
Canada  v6k 4s2
www.davidsuzuki.org
contact@davidsuzuki.org
Tel: 604-732-4228
Fax: 604-732-0752

Checks can be made payable to The David Suzuki Foundation.
All donations are tax-deductible.
Canadian charitable registration: (BN) 12775 6716 RR0001
U.S. charitable registration: #94-3204049

DEC    2009

OCT    2012